Starting Out or Starting Over

An Expert's Checklists for Life's Major Decisions

James M. Kramon
Attorney at Law

SPHINX® PUBLISHING
AN IMPRINT OF SOURCEBOOKS, INC.®
NAPERVILLE, ILLINOIS
www.SphinxLegal.com

Copyright © 2004 by James M. Kramon
Cover and internal design © 2004 by Sourcebooks, Inc.

All rights reserved. No part of this book may be reproduced in any form or by any electronic or mechanical means including information storage and retrieval systems—except in the case of brief quotations embodied in critical articles or reviews—without permission in writing from its publisher, Sourcebooks, Inc.® Purchasers of the book are granted a license to use the forms contained herein for their own personal use. No claim of copyright is made in any government form reproduced herein.

First Edition: 2004

Published by: **Sphinx® Publishing, An Imprint of Sourcebooks, Inc.®**

Naperville Office
P. O. Box 4410
Naperville, Illinois 60567-4410
630-961-3900
Fax: 630-961-2168
www.sourcebooks.com
www.SphinxLegal.com

This publication is designed to provide accurate and authoritative information in regard to the subject matter covered. It is sold with the understanding that the publisher is not engaged in rendering legal, accounting, or other professional service. If legal advice or other expert assistance is required, the services of a competent professional person should be sought.

From a Declaration of Principles Jointly Adopted by a Committee of the American Bar Association and a Committee of Publishers and Associations

This product is not a substitute for legal advice.

Disclaimer required by Texas statutes.

Library of Congress Cataloging-in-Publication Data

Kramon, James M.
  Starting out or starting over : an expert's checklists for life's major decisions / by James M. Kramon.-- 1st ed.
     p. cm.
  Includes index.
  ISBN 1-57248-454-3
  1. Law--United States--Popular works. 2. Finance, Personal--United States--Popular works. I. Title.

KF387.K73 2004
332.024--dc22
                                                                2004018384

Printed and bound in the United States of America.

VP — 10 9 8 7 6 5 4 3 2 1

Dedication

To Paula, who conceived this book, and to Justin and Annie.

Acknowledgement

I would like to thank my wife who suggested this book at the time our son was completing college and our daughter was finishing high school. Paula, for your ideas and encouragement, and Justin and Annie, for your thoughts and questions, I am greatly indebted.

Many thanks are due to my agent, Julia Lord, for her tireless efforts and invaluable suggestions throughout the writing of this book.

To my close friends, Barbara Dale and John Weiss, I owe thanks for their useful ideas and constructive criticisms.

The help of Valerie Lazzaro of American Express Tax and Business Services with tax matters discussed in this book is much appreciated.

It has been a privilege and pleasure to work with my editors, Dianne Wheeler and Michael Bowen, at Sphinx/SourceBooks.

As usual, I could not have completed this book without the assistance and hard work of Nancy Sumwalt. Nancy organized every chapter of this book and always let me know when I missed the mark.

Contents

Introduction xi

Section I: The Basics—Work and Money

Chapter 1: Your Job 3
  Employment Contracts
  Terms Used in Employment Contracts
  Checklist for Employment Contracts
  Employment Benefits
  Checklist of Employment Benefits
  Paperwork for New Employees
  Checklist for New Employees
  Form W-4
  Changing Employment
  Checklist for Ending Employment

Chapter 2: Managing Finances 29
  Checklist for Managing Your Finances
  Addresses for Major Credit Reporting Agencies
  How to Handle Your Checking Account
  Checklist of Dos and Don'ts for Checking Accounts
  Terms Used in Banking
  Tax-Qualified Retirement Plans
  Types of Retirement Plans
  Things to Do to Provide for Possible Death or Disability
  Checklist of Things to Do to Provide for Possible Death or Disability

Chapter 3: Your Income Taxes............53
Terms Used in Income Tax Matters
Free Publications from the IRS
Federal Tax Rates
FICA (Social Security and Medicare)
W-2s and 1099s
Form W-2
Form 1099
Filing Tax Returns
Checklist for Preparing for Tax Time
Selecting and Using an Accountant or Other Tax Preparer
   Sample Fax to an Accountant
   Sample Response Fax from an Accountant
   Sample Email to an Accountant
   Sample Response Email from an Accountant
Dealing with the IRS and State Taxing Authorities

Section II: The Necessities—Home and Car

Chapter 4: Renting An Apartment...............79
Finding an Apartment
Checklist for Finding an Apartment
Dealing with Real Estate Brokers
Checklist for Dealing with Real Estate Brokers
Your Lease
Terms Used in Leases
Checklist for Your Lease
Complaints and Requests
Checklist for Complaints and Requests
   Sample Complaint Letter to Landlord
Dealing with a Roommate
Checklist for Dealing with a Roommate

Apartment Insurance
Terms Used in Apartment Insurance Policies
Checklist for Apartment Insurance
Making a Claim under Your Apartment Insurance Policy
Checklist for Making a Claim under Your Apartment Insurance Policy
Sample Letter to Apartment Insurance Company

Chapter 5: Automobiles 103
Should I Buy a Car?
Checklist of Costs of Owning a Car
Buying a Car
Checklist for Buying a Car
Financing the Purchase of a Car
Car Inspections
Checklist for Car Inspections
Automobile Insurance
Checklist of Components of Automobile Insurance
Accidents
Checklist for Handling Accidents

Chapter 6: Buying A House 125
Checklist for Buying a House
Terms Used in Buying a House
Contract to Buy a House
Checklist for Contract to Buy a House
Homeowners Insurance
Checklist for Homeowners Insurance
Closing
Checklist for House Closing
Repairs and Improvements to Your House

Section III: The Essentials—Insurance and Medical Care

Chapter 7: Liability Insurance 161
Checklist for Obtaining Liability Insurance

Chapter 8: Medical Care 169
Checklist of Types of Medical Insurance
Selecting an HMO
Terms Used in HMO Provider Agreements
Checklist of Factors to Consider in Selecting an HMO
   Sample Worksheet for Comparing HMOs
Forming a Relationship with Your HMO
Checklist for Forming a Relationship with Your HMO
Specialists, Testing, Drugs, and Other Medical Care
Checklist for Obtaining Specialists, Testing, Drugs,
   and Other Medical Care
Resolving Disputes
Checklist for Resolving Disputes with Your HMO
   Sample Letter to HMO that Refuses to Provide a Specialist

Chapter 9: Life and Disability Insurance 207
Terms Used in Life Insurance Policies
Checklist for Purchasing Life Insurance
Disability Insurance
Checklist of Possible Sources of Money in the Event of Disability
Terms Used in Disability Insurance Policies
How to Obtain Disability Insurance
Checklist for Obtaining a Disability Insurance Policy
Making a Claim for Disability Benefits

Section IV: The Lessons—Resolving Problems

Chapter 10: Buying Goods and Services 231
Checklist for What a Contract to Buy Goods should Include
Contract to Buy Services
Checklist for Contract to Buy Services
Guarantees and Warranties
Checklist for Guarantees and Warranties
    Sample Letter to Someone Who is Selling Goods to You
    Sample Letter to Someone Who is Providing Services to You

Chapter 11: Resolving Disputes 245
Checklist of Ways to Avoid Disputes
Handling Legal Disputes
Checklist for Writing a Legal Letter
    Sample Letter Regarding Defective Repairs
    Sample Letter to Bank Regarding Checking Account
    Sample Letter Requesting Approval to See a Specialist
    Sample Letter Regarding Lack of Trash Removal Services

Conclusion 261
Index 263
About the Author 268

Introduction

The purpose of this book is to enable you to handle the legal and business matters that arise in your life with confidence. This is not a book about theories or philosophies of life. It is a book about precisely what you need to know to enter a good lease for an apartment, buy a car or house, get the most out of your job, choose insurance that is useful and cost-effective, manage your taxes, and do the other things that, if you had a family fortune and a good lawyer at your disposal, you would not need to worry about. The idea of this book is to provide you with precise instructions for the legal and business matters you need to address. The instructions are complete and contain checklists that are easy to follow and fully explained. I have used these methods for over thirty years with hundreds of clients.

It is a lawyer's world out there. Lawyers make the law, interpret it, and enforce it. They determine what you can and cannot do. In every situation you will face, lawyers set the stage, choose the actors, and direct the play. They prepare the leases, contracts, insurance policies, employment agreements, tax documents, guaranties, and every other oversized document that is handed to you. It is no wonder that the documents the average person is expected to go through in ordinary life convince many people that lawyers get paid for their work by the word. While this is not exactly accurate, it is absolutely true that lawyers benefit from length and complexity even when they serve no purpose.

Lawyers are masters at making things complicated and adversarial. If you look at a lease, insurance policy, employment contract, or any of the documents you get from banks, credit card companies, hospitals, or just about anyone else you need to deal with, you will find more words than in the Treaty of Paris. This country was able to achieve independence with less on paper than one person needs today to get a mortgage or lease a car.

So where does this book come in? Since lawyers are responsible for making these matters so difficult in the first place, I thought at least one of us should show you how to get these things done correctly without spending your life on them or exhausting your finances. This book shows you how to get what you want in spite of these hardships. It shows you how to play on a playing field designed by lawyers without getting mowed down every time you pick up the ball. It shows you how to separate the things you want and need from mountains of garbage that serve only to confuse. Once you learn the cut-to-the-chase method this book demonstrates, you will be able to hold your own with anyone you have to deal with in your everyday life.

Many lawyers work on a *checklist* approach. This approach enables a lawyer to keep track of the things that are important to a client and be sure that each one of them is handled correctly. If your checklist is complete and straightforward, and you do not skip any of the items on it, you end up with the result you need.

Each item on every checklist is explained so that you can fully understand it. Where a particular item on a checklist has several parts, I have sometimes broken the item down in a follow-up checklist, to be sure you understand every necessary step. When a checklist is not the best way to explain something—such as when there is only one thing to do in a particular situation and you need to understand the best way to do it—a simple explanation for that matter is provided. For example, when you get to the chapter about automobiles, you will find checklists for determining the cost of a car, steps to follow when you buy a car, items to include in your car insurance, and precisely what to do if you have an accident. You will also find some information about inspections and the financing of cars. You can select the items that are of importance to you at a particular time or, if you wish, you can read the whole chapter when you are thinking about getting a car.

Either way, this book is organized to give you the information you need in the shortest and most convenient form. I have included explanations of terms that may not be familiar, as well as some forms and letters that may be useful in various matters.

Section I

The Basics
Work and Money

CHAPTER 1

Your Job

An *employee* is a person hired by an employer to work on an ongoing basis. Employees must do the work the employer hires them to do and they are subject to the employer's directions about how to do the work. Employers take tax and other deductions out of the employees' pay and they arrange for unemployment insurance and worker's compensation insurance as required by state law.

Independent contractors are workers hired for specific pieces of work only. If you are a plumber and do not work for a plumbing company on a regular basis, you are an independent contractor. The person who hires an independent contractor does not tell him or her how to do the work. An independent contractor plumber, for example, could be hired to fit out the bathrooms in a house. He would install the sinks, toilets, showers, and bathtubs in accordance with the plans, get his fee, and go on to other work. He would not be an employee and would not have an employment contract. Tax and other deductions are not taken out of the pay of independent contractors.

For various reasons, government agencies prefer people to be employees rather than independent contractors. One of the reasons is that employers are required to deduct and pay income taxes for employees to the federal and state governments. Independent contractors do not have such income tax deductions taken from their pay and they must pay their income taxes themselves, generally four times a year.

Employment Contracts

This chapter focuses on the employer-employee relationship, not an employer-independant contractor. However, much of the information regarding what an employment contract should contain, what benefits are important, and how to change jobs can be applied to an independant contractor situation as well.

There are different types of employment contracts. Some are oral and some are written. The written contracts vary from a simple employer letter, confirming that you are hired on particular terms, to a fairly lengthy written document, known generally as an *Employment Agreement* or *Employment Contract*. In the simplest employment contract, there are three basic matters agreed upon:

1. the work description (what you will be doing);
2. the salary (what you will be paid); and,
3. the term (how long you will be doing the work).

When no specific term of employment is agreed upon, the employment contract is known as an *at-will employment contract*. In this type of employment contract, the employer can fire you at any time, for any reason (other than because you exercise a right protected by law or because of unlawful discrimination). Likewise, you can quit at any time, for any reason.

At the other extreme, some employment contracts are very complicated, covering all sorts of items. As a general rule, your employment contract becomes more complicated as the job gets better, but this is not always the case. People are hired as presidents of fair-sized companies with no written employment contract, while others are hired, all the time, as entry-level employees for large companies that require them to sign complicated employment contracts.

The average person has nothing to say about what kind of contract the employer requires for a particular job—but everything to say about the terms of his or her employment contract. Although employers may seem a lot bigger and wealthier than you are, you have one absolute bargaining chip—you can walk out the door!

If your employment contract is oral, ask enough questions and gain enough understanding so that you are comfortable going to work. If your employment contract is written, review it carefully and do not be shy about asking questions and requesting changes.

A number of companies have policy manuals or employee handbooks that are considered to be a part of every employee's employment contract. A number of companies require employees to sign receipts confirming that they have received a copy of the policy manual or employee handbook. These materials usually cover a wide range of subjects, from what you are required to do if something improper occurs to dress codes. Generally, written employment contracts specifically mention these items as well. Whether or not you have a written employment contract, find out whether your employer provides any such materials and, if so, familiarize yourself with them.

The best way to proceed if you have questions about your employment contract or do not understand if it covers a particular matter is to ask the appropriate person at your company. In a large company, there will be designated people available for this purpose. In smaller companies, you will have to figure out the best person to ask. If you have an immediate supervisor, start with that person, because you may offend him or her if you unnecessarily go above his or her head. Never be afraid to ask respectful questions about your employment contract. It is one of the things that affects your life greatly and you are entitled to fully understand it.

Terms Used in Employment Contracts

- **annual leave.** Time off from work for vacations and personal reasons.
- **at-will employment.** An employment contract with no specific term of employment.
- **benefits.** Things other than salary, such as medical insurance, that you receive through your employer.
- **commission.** A payment by an employer that is based upon the amount an employee sells.
- **deductions.** Federal and state taxes, FICA (Social Security and Medicare), and other costs taken out of your salary.
- **draw.** A periodic advance payment by the employer that is credited to commissions to be earned.
- **employee.** A person who is working for an employer.
- **employer.** A person or business that is hiring an employee.
- **expenses.** Money spent in the course of performing a job.
- **extension term (renewal term).** An additional period of time for which an employee may be employed.
- **for cause.** Action an employer may take because of something an employee does.
- **not for cause.** Action an employer may take regardless of what the employee does.
- **restrictive covenant.** An agreement by an employee not to engage in certain employment for a period time after working for the employer.
- **salary.** The pay an employee receives for his or her work.
- **sick leave.** Time off from work because of illness or injury.
- **term.** The time period for which an employee is employed.
- **termination.** The ending of the employment relationship.

Checklist for Employment Contracts

- ❏ Correct job description or duties
- ❏ Acceptable job title
- ❏ Acceptable salary and frequency of payments
- ❏ Agreed upon benefits
- ❏ Employer's rights to terminate your employment
- ❏ Your rights to terminate your employment
- ❏ Acceptable annual leave, personal leave, and sick leave
- ❏ No unacceptable change in your work allowed
- ❏ Any postemployment restrictions

✔ Correct job description or duties

Review your employment contract carefully to see how it describes your job duties. The employment contract should say what it is you are going to be doing when you go to work for the employer. If this part of the employment contract does not exactly fit your understanding of what you are being hired to do, have it addressed and agreed to before you sign the contract. If there are things you are not going to be doing in your job, be sure that those are mentioned as well. For example, if you are hired as a full-time truck driver for an interstate moving company, but it is understood that you will not be loading and unloading the trucks, that fact should be stated in your employment contract.

✔ Acceptable job title

Your job title may or may not be important to you.

If you are insistent on having a particular place on the corporate ladder, or if getting a job later depends on your job title today, this matter becomes important. It also may be important with regard to the progression of your salary and benefits. For example, a job title such as Vice President or Plant Manager may be important to you, because such a title may establish where you stand in a company relative to other employees as well as your entitlement to certain benefits.

☑ Acceptable salary and frequency of payments

Verify the salary that is being provided to you and the pay periods that apply (bi-weekly, monthly, etc.). If you are being paid on a *commission* basis, check the wording carefully so that you understand how much you will be paid and when you will be paid. In many employment contracts, commissions are not paid until the employer has been paid by the customer. If this is the case, you will obviously have to wait different periods of time to receive your commissions.

In other employment contracts, the employee gets a certain amount of money each pay period, known as a *draw*, and the exact commission is reconciled periodically. Be sure in any commission arrangement that your employment contract indicates an acceptable time frame for you to be paid. Of course, any provision in the employment contract for future raises should be carefully reviewed.

☑ Agreed upon benefits

Possible *benefits* range from different forms of insurance to different types of paid leave to reimbursement for particular expenses. There are many types of benefits, so a checklist is provided later in this chapter to help you review this matter carefully. (see p. 11.)

☑ Employer's rights to terminate your employment

If your employment contract is an at-will employment contract, you may be terminated at any time and for any reason, except to punish you for exercising protected rights or to discriminate against you. For example, your employer cannot fire you because of your age, sex, color, national origin, sexual preference, physical condition unrelated to the job, or religion. You also cannot be fired because you speak out about important public issues.

The majority of employment contracts—up to middle-range ($50,000–$100,000) salary employment contracts—are at-will employment contracts. In more complicated employment contracts, a distinction is generally made between *for cause* terminations and *not for cause* terminations. For cause simply means that there is a reason for the termination based upon an employee's conduct. Not for cause means this is not so. Some employment contracts define *cause* rather precisely, such as the commission of a crime or failure to obey the company's rules.

✓ Your rights to terminate your employment

If your employment contract is an at-will employment contract, you can terminate your employment at any time. It is customary to give one week's notice or one pay period's notice. Since you generally want a good reference from past employers, it makes sense to give enough notice so that an employer feels it has been treated satisfactorily. Your contract may require you to give a certain amount of notice if you wish to end your employment.

✓ Acceptable annual leave, personal leave, and sick leave

Unfortunately, employment contracts in the United States often provide far too little *annual leave*. It is not uncommon in this country to see employers that provide only one week's annual leave for the first year. This is a bargaining matter, of course, but you might want to be aware that in many countries, much more annual leave is provided from the outset and, in fact, there are countries that require employees to use that leave.

Sick leave is also important. It should be defined so that you can use it with reasonable discretion when you require it. Some employers require a doctor's note before certain amounts of sick leave are utilized. (This is distrustful of employees and you should try to avoid it if you can.) Your employment contract should indicate that you will receive your regular pay when you are taking either annual leave, personal leave, or sick leave.

 No unacceptable change in your work allowed
If your employer has numerous locations and only one particular location is acceptable to you, your employment contract should indicate that your work location will not be changed. If your employer has various hours of work, be sure that your contract indicates what hours have been agreed upon. If there are any other conditions of your work that you insist not be changed, get those stated in your employment contract as well.

 Any postemployment restrictions
Review your employment contract to see whether it places any restrictions on you while you are employed by your employer or after you leave. Some employment contracts restrict the employee's right to do any work except for the employer, and some restrict the employee's right to do work after the contract is over. These restrictions, which are known as *restrictive covenants*, are sometimes dangerous because they may limit your right to work someplace else at a later time. If you violate a restrictive covenant, you could wind up in a lawsuit that would not be much fun. In addition, employers who hire people who have worked for a company known to have a restrictive covenant in its employment contract often require those employees to prove that they will not be violating the restrictive covenant if they work for the new employer.

• • • • •

Employment Benefits

There are many different benefits provided by employers. Some benefits are unusual, such as the use of particular vacation facilities, but most benefits fall into the following categories.

Checklist of Employment Benefits

- ❏ Medical insurance
- ❏ Life insurance
- ❏ Disability insurance
- ❏ Paid annual and personal leave
- ❏ Paid sick leave
- ❏ Car use or mileage reimbursement
- ❏ Business expense reimbursement
- ❏ Payments to a retirement plan
- ❏ Facility use
- ❏ Flexible spending plan use

 Medical insurance

Since medical insurance is often regarded as the most important employment benefit, be sure that your employment contract is specific about what medical insurance you will be eligible for and what portion of its cost will be paid by your employer. Some medical insurance plans include dental and vision expenses.

 Life insurance

Various employers provide a certain amount of life insurance in one form or another. (The difference between whole life insurance and term life insurance is explained in Chapter 9.) If your employer provides life insurance, be sure to designate the beneficiary you want to receive the life insurance money in the event of your death.

Disability insurance

There are two general types of disability insurance—*short-term* and *long-term*. Short-term disability insurance covers your inability to work for relatively brief periods of time, generally between ninety days and one year. Long-term disability insurance covers your inability to work for substantial periods of time, sometimes until you reach the age of retirement, which is usually 65, and occasionally for the rest of your life. (The concerns you need to address with regard to disability insurance are explained in Chapter 9.)

Paid annual and personal leave

Employers provide regular employees with certain amounts of leave for vacations and for any personal purposes such as deaths within the employee's family. Obviously, the more such leave your employment agreement provides the better. You should be paid your normal wages during leave. A question that may arise is whether any unused annual or personal leave becomes available during the next year or if it is simply lost. This is something to look into if you plan on not using all of your annual or personal leave in a particular year.

Paid sick leave

Employers differ on whether the use of sick leave requires documentation from a physician or not. It is unreasonable to require documentation for one or two days of sick leave for colds and flus. You should receive your regular wages during such leave time and also determine whether unused portions of such leave carry over to the next year.

Car use or mileage reimbursement

If you use your own car in your work, your employer should reimburse you for doing so. Often, the reimbursement is at the rate set by the IRS for tax-deduction purposes. The rate as of January 1, 2004 is 37.5¢ per mile, but it changes from year to year. Of course, to the extent that you are reimbursed by your employer, you cannot claim a tax deduction.

Employers in some instances provide employees with a car for their use. If this occurs, you will need to separate the business and personal parts of the use of that car for tax purposes. An accountant or tax preparer can easily show you how to do this.

Business expense reimbursement

An employee's *business expenses* may range from travel, accommodations, meals, and work clothes, to simple things, such as inexpensive supplies. If your job is going to require you to expend money, you will want to be certain that your employment contract provides for reimbursement.

Payments to a retirement plan

The various types of retirement plans and the possibility of employer contributions are explained in Chapter 2.

Facility use

Some employers provide employees with the use of certain facilities for the employer's purpose and some provide employees with the use of certain facilities as an employment benefit. Such facilities may include restaurants or health clubs.

☑ Flexible spending plan use

Tax laws permit employers to establish what are known as *Flexible Spending Accounts* for medical care, dependent care, and transportation expenses (mass transit and parking). These accounts reimburse employees for these particular expenses and use before-tax dollars contributed by the employee for such purposes. The funds in Flexible Spending Accounts come from deductions from an employee's salary, and the amounts deducted are not taxed. The catch is that you have to determine in advance of each plan year how much of your salary you want deducted for each purpose. If you fail to utilize the money available in a tax year, you lose it.

If you are certain that you will spend a particular amount on these expenses, a Flexible Spending Account is obviously a no-brainer if your employer offers one. Review the plan, however, before you elect to have money deducted from your paycheck for it. You will find that there are specific requirements regarding filing claims for payment from your plan account.

• • • • •

Paperwork For New Employees

When you get a job, there is a lot of paperwork to be completed. Some of it is for the benefit of your employer and some of it is required by various government agencies. As long as the information that is requested is reasonable and easily available to you, you do not need to be concerned about supplying it. However, you do need to understand the various choices that a new employee must make, since they can affect your pocketbook in various ways.

Here is a checklist of things to do when you get a new job. A conscientious employer will have a person designated to go over these things with you. Do not be shy about asking questions.

Checklist for New Employees

- ❑ Claim the desired number of dependents on your Form W-4
- ❑ Verify that you are properly covered by workers' compensation insurance and unemployment insurance
- ❑ Designate beneficiaries for retirement plans and insurance policies
- ❑ Review any employment manuals, handbooks, or recent memoranda to employees
- ❑ Make any elections required by your retirement plan
- ❑ Familiarize yourself with your rights as an employee
- ❑ Know that every employee is entitled to work in a safe and healthy work environment
- ❑ Arrange to have your employer deposit your salary directly into your checking account

☑ Claim the desired number of dependents on your Form W-4

One of the tax forms you will be completing is known as a *Form W-4*. On this form, you must designate the number of dependents for whom you claim to be responsible. A *dependent* is someone you take care of financially most of the time. Unless your situation is highly unusual and someone else is financially responsible for you most of the time, you are your own dependent. If you are married, your spouse may or may not be your dependent, but if you are filing a joint tax return it does not matter. A child being cared for is a dependent of one or both parents.

The more dependents you claim, the less money is taken out in taxes each pay period from your pay check. Do not claim more than you are allowed, as there could be consequences for doing so with the IRS. You are not required to claim all of your dependents. You might, for example, claim "0" dependents when you are entitled to claim "1" for yourself. Since the fewer dependents you claim, the greater the deductions your employer will take for federal and state taxes, you may want to claim less dependents in order to get some money back at income tax time. On the other hand, extra *deductions* on your tax return, such as high mortgage interest, may entitle you to claim extra exemptions on your Form W-4. You can determine with tax tables that are available from your employer, any accountant, or a tax preparer what your income taxes will be with different numbers of dependents. With this information, you can decide the best number of dependents for you to claim.

> *The form your employer will give you to fill out will look like the example on the following page. You will also be required to complete a state form regarding your claimed number of dependents. You can do your computation for this form in exactly the same manner.*

Your Job **17**

Form W-4 (2004)

Purpose. Complete Form W-4 so that your employer can withhold the correct Federal income tax from your pay. Because your tax situation may change, you may want to refigure your withholding each year.

Exemption from withholding. If you are exempt, complete only lines 1, 2, 3, 4, and 7 and sign the form to validate it. Your exemption for 2004 expires February 16, 2005. See **Pub. 505,** Tax Withholding and Estimated Tax.

Note: *You cannot claim exemption from withholding if: (a) your income exceeds $800 and includes more than $250 of unearned income (e.g., interest and dividends) and (b) another person can claim you as a dependent on their tax return.*

Basic instructions. If you are not exempt, complete the **Personal Allowances Worksheet** below. The worksheets on page 2 adjust your withholding allowances based on itemized deductions, certain credits, adjustments to income, or two-earner/two-job situations. Complete all worksheets that apply. **However, you may claim fewer (or zero) allowances.**

Head of household. Generally, you may claim head of household filing status on your tax return only if you are unmarried and pay more than 50% of the costs of keeping up a home for yourself and your dependent(s) or other qualifying individuals. See line E below.

Tax credits. You can take projected tax credits into account in figuring your allowable number of withholding allowances. Credits for child or dependent care expenses and the child tax credit may be claimed using the **Personal Allowances Worksheet** below. See Pub. 919, How Do I Adjust My Tax Withholding? for information on converting your other credits into withholding allowances.

Nonwage income. If you have a large amount of nonwage income, such as interest or dividends, consider making estimated tax payments using **Form 1040-ES,** Estimated Tax for Individuals. Otherwise, you may owe additional tax.

Two earners/two jobs. If you have a working spouse or more than one job, figure the total number of allowances you are entitled to claim on all jobs using worksheets from only one Form W-4. Your withholding usually will be most accurate when all allowances are claimed on the Form W-4 for the highest paying job and zero allowances are claimed on the others.

Nonresident alien. If you are a nonresident alien, see the **Instructions for Form 8233** before completing this Form W-4.

Check your withholding. After your Form W-4 takes effect, use Pub. 919 to see how the dollar amount you are having withheld compares to your projected total tax for 2004. See Pub. 919, especially if your earnings exceed $125,000 (Single) or $175,000 (Married).

Recent name change? If your name on line 1 differs from that shown on your social security card, call 1-800-772-1213 to initiate a name change and obtain a social security card showing your correct name.

Personal Allowances Worksheet (Keep for your records.)

A   Enter "1" for **yourself** if no one else can claim you as a dependent . . . . A _____

B   Enter "1" if: { • You are single and have only one job; or
 • You are married, have only one job, and your spouse does not work; or
 • Your wages from a second job or your spouse's wages (or the total of both) are $1,000 or less. } . . B _____

C   Enter "1" for your **spouse.** But, you may choose to enter "-0-" if you are married and have either a working spouse or more than one job. (Entering "-0-" may help you avoid having too little tax withheld.) . . . . C _____

D   Enter number of **dependents** (other than your spouse or yourself) you will claim on your tax return . . . . D _____

E   Enter "1" if you will file as **head of household** on your tax return (see conditions under **Head of household** above) . E _____

F   Enter "1" if you have at least $1,500 of **child or dependent care expenses** for which you plan to claim a credit . . F _____
    (**Note: Do not** include child support payments. See **Pub. 503,** Child and Dependent Care Expenses, for details.)

G   **Child Tax Credit** (including additional child tax credit):
 • If your total income will be less than $52,000 ($77,000 if married), enter "2" for each eligible child.
 • If your total income will be between $52,000 and $84,000 ($77,000 and $119,000 if married), enter "1" for each eligible child plus "1" **additional** if you have four or more eligible children.   G _____

H   Add lines A through G and enter total here. **Note:** *This may be different from the number of exemptions you claim on your tax return.* ▶ H _____

For accuracy, complete all worksheets that apply.
 • If you plan to **itemize or claim adjustments to income** and want to reduce your withholding, see the **Deductions and Adjustments Worksheet** on page 2.
 • If you have **more than one job** or are **married** and you and your spouse **both work** and the combined earnings from all jobs exceed $35,000 ($25,000 if married) see the **Two-Earner/Two-Job Worksheet** on page 2 to avoid having too little tax withheld.
 • If **neither** of the above situations applies, **stop here** and enter the number from line H on line 5 of Form W-4 below.

- - - - - - - - - - - - - - - - Cut here and give Form W-4 to your employer. Keep the top part for your records. - - - - - - - - - - - - - - - -

Form **W-4**
Department of the Treasury
Internal Revenue Service

Employee's Withholding Allowance Certificate

▶ Your employer must send a copy of this form to the IRS if: (a) you claim more than 10 allowances or (b) you claim "Exempt" and your wages are normally more than $200 per week.

OMB No. 1545-0010

2004

1	Type or print your first name and middle initial	Last name		2	Your social security number
	Home address (number and street or rural route)		3 ☐ Single ☐ Married ☐ Married, but withhold at higher Single rate.		
			Note: *If married, but legally separated, or spouse is a nonresident alien, check the "Single" box.*		
	City or town, state, and ZIP code		4 If your last name differs from that shown on your social security card, check here. You must call 1-800-772-1213 for a new card. ▶ ☐		

5   Total number of allowances you are claiming (from line **H** above **or** from the applicable worksheet on page 2)   **5** _____
6   Additional amount, if any, you want withheld from each paycheck . . . . **6** $ _____
7   I claim exemption from withholding for 2004, and I certify that I meet **both** of the following conditions for exemption:
 • Last year I had a right to a refund of **all** Federal income tax withheld because I had **no** tax liability **and**
 • This year I expect a refund of **all** Federal income tax withheld because I expect to have **no** tax liability.
 If you meet both conditions, write "Exempt" here . . . . ▶ | **7** |

Under penalties of perjury, I certify that I am entitled to the number of withholding allowances claimed on this certificate, or I am entitled to claim exempt status.
Employee's signature
(Form is not valid unless you sign it.) ▶ _____   Date ▶ _____

8	Employer's name and address (Employer: Complete lines 8 and 10 only if sending to the IRS.)	9	Office code (optional)	10	Employer identification number (EIN)

For Privacy Act and Paperwork Reduction Act Notice, see page 2.   Cat. No. 10220Q   Form **W-4** (2004)

18 Starting Out or Starting Over

Form W-4 (2004) Page **2**

Deductions and Adjustments Worksheet

Note: *Use this worksheet **only** if you plan to itemize deductions, claim certain credits, or claim adjustments to income on your 2004 tax return.*

1. Enter an estimate of your 2004 itemized deductions. These include qualifying home mortgage interest, charitable contributions, state and local taxes, medical expenses in excess of 7.5% of your income, and miscellaneous deductions. (For 2004, you may have to reduce your itemized deductions if your income is over $142,700 ($71,350 if married filing separately). See **Worksheet 3** in Pub. 919 for details.) . . . **1** $ _____

2. Enter:
   - $9,700 if married filing jointly or qualifying widow(er)
   - $7,150 if head of household
   - $4,850 if single
   - $4,850 if married filing separately

   . . . . **2** $ _____

3. **Subtract** line 2 from line 1. If line 2 is greater than line 1, enter "-0-". . . . . **3** $ _____
4. Enter an estimate of your 2004 adjustments to income, including alimony, deductible IRA contributions, and student loan interest **4** $ _____
5. **Add** lines 3 and 4 and enter the total. (Include any amount for credits from **Worksheet 7** in Pub. 919) . **5** $ _____
6. Enter an estimate of your 2004 nonwage income (such as dividends or interest) . . . . **6** $ _____
7. **Subtract** line 6 from line 5. Enter the result, but not less than "-0-". . . . . **7** $ _____
8. **Divide** the amount on line 7 by $3,000 and enter the result here. Drop any fraction . . . . . **8** _____
9. Enter the number from the **Personal Allowances Worksheet,** line H, page 1 . . . . **9** _____
10. **Add** lines 8 and 9 and enter the total here. If you plan to use the **Two-Earner/Two-Job Worksheet,** also enter this total on line 1 below. Otherwise, **stop here** and enter this total on Form W-4, line 5, page 1 . **10** _____

Two-Earner/Two-Job Worksheet (See **Two earners/two jobs** on page 1.)

Note: *Use this worksheet **only** if the instructions under line H on page 1 direct you here.*

1. Enter the number from line H, page 1 (or from line 10 above if you used the **Deductions and Adjustments Worksheet**) **1** _____
2. Find the number in **Table 1** below that applies to the **LOWEST** paying job and enter it here . . . . **2** _____
3. If line 1 is **more than or equal to** line 2, subtract line 2 from line 1. Enter the result here (if zero, enter "-0-") and on Form W-4, line 5, page 1. **Do not** use the rest of this worksheet . . . . **3** _____

Note: *If line 1 is **less than** line 2, enter "-0-" on Form W-4, line 5, page 1. Complete lines 4-9 below to calculate the additional withholding amount necessary to avoid a year-end tax bill.*

4. Enter the number from line 2 of this worksheet . . . . **4** _____
5. Enter the number from line 1 of this worksheet . . . . **5** _____
6. **Subtract** line 5 from line 4 . . . . **6** _____
7. Find the amount in **Table 2** below that applies to the **HIGHEST** paying job and enter it here . . . **7** $ _____
8. **Multiply** line 7 by line 6 and enter the result here. This is the additional annual withholding needed . **8** $ _____
9. Divide line 8 by the number of pay periods remaining in 2004. For example, divide by 26 if you are paid every two weeks and you complete this form in December 2003. Enter the result here and on Form W-4, line 6, page 1. This is the additional amount to be withheld from each paycheck . . . . **9** $ _____

Table 1: Two-Earner/Two-Job Worksheet

Married Filing Jointly			Married Filing Jointly			All Others	
If wages from HIGHEST paying job are-	AND, wages from LOWEST paying job are-	Enter on line 2 above	If wages from HIGHEST paying job are-	AND, wages from LOWEST paying job are-	Enter on line 2 above	If wages from LOWEST paying job are-	Enter on line 2 above
$0 - $40,000	$0 - $4,000	0	$40,001 and over	31,001 - 38,000	6	$0 - $6,000	0
	4,001 - 8,000	1		38,001 - 44,000	7	6,001 - 11,000	1
	8,001 - 17,000	2		44,001 - 50,000	8	11,001 - 18,000	2
	17,001 and over	3		50,001 - 55,000	9	18,001 - 25,000	3
				55,001 - 65,000	10	25,001 - 31,000	4
$40,001 and over	$0 - $4,000	0		65,001 - 75,000	11	31,001 - 44,000	5
	4,001 - 8,000	1		75,001 - 85,000	12	44,001 - 55,000	6
	8,001 - 15,000	2		85,001 - 100,000	13	55,001 - 70,000	7
	15,001 - 22,000	3		100,001 - 115,000	14	70,001 - 80,000	8
	22,001 - 25,000	4		115,001 and over	15	80,001 - 100,000	9
	25,001 - 31,000	5				100,001 and over	10

Table 2: Two-Earner/Two-Job Worksheet

Married Filing Jointly		All Others	
If wages from HIGHEST paying job are-	Enter on line 7 above	If wages from HIGHEST paying job are-	Enter on line 7 above
$0 - $60,000	$470	$0 - $30,000	$470
60,001 - 110,000	780	30,001 - 70,000	780
110,001 - 150,000	870	70,001 - 140,000	870
150,001 - 270,000	1,020	140,001 - 320,000	1,020
270,001 and over	1,090	320,001 and over	1,090

Privacy Act and Paperwork Reduction Act Notice. We ask for the information on this form to carry out the Internal Revenue laws of the United States. The Internal Revenue Code requires this information under sections 3402(f)(2)(A) and 6109 and their regulations. **Failure to provide a properly completed form will result in your being treated as a single person who claims no withholding allowances;** providing fraudulent information may also subject you to penalties. Routine uses of this information include giving it to the Department of Justice for civil and criminal litigation, to cities, states, and the District of Columbia for use in administering their tax laws, and using it in the National Directory of New Hires. We may also disclose this information to Federal and state agencies to enforce Federal nontax criminal laws and to combat terrorism.

You are not required to provide the information requested on a form that is subject to the Paperwork Reduction Act unless the form displays a valid OMB control number. Books or records relating to a form or its instructions must be retained as long as their contents may become material in the administration of any Internal Revenue law. Generally, tax returns and return information are confidential, as required by Code section 6103.

The time needed to complete this form will vary depending on individual circumstances. The estimated average time is: **Recordkeeping,** 46 min.; **Learning about the law or the form,** 13 min.; **Preparing the form,** 59 min. If you have comments concerning the accuracy of these time estimates or suggestions for making this form simpler, we would be happy to hear from you. You can write to the Tax Products Coordinating Committee, Western Area Distribution Center, Rancho Cordova, CA 95743-0001. **Do not** send Form W-4 to this address. Instead, give it to your employer.

☑ Verify that you are properly covered by workers' compensation insurance and unemployment insurance

State law requires employers to have workers' compensation insurance and unemployment insurance for their employees. Your employer can easily verify that you are included in the roster of employees for these purposes. Workers' compensation insurance provides employees with protection if they are injured or become ill as a result of their employment. Unemployment insurance provides employees with a certain amount of compensation for a certain period of time (frequently twenty-six weeks) if they lose their jobs through no fault of their own. State commissions are available to hear both workers' compensation and unemployment claims. Some states require self-employed individuals to maintain one or both of these forms of insurance.

☑ Designate beneficiaries for retirement plans and insurance policies

If you die during the time you are employed, the vested rights in your retirement funds and proceeds of life insurance policies will be payable to designated individuals. (The meaning of vested rights is explained in Chapter 2. An explanation of being a beneficiary of a life insurance policy occurs in Chapter 9.) Often, people designate spouses, significant others, or other family members to receive these funds upon their death. Most retirement plans and life insurance policies make it possible to select a *primary* beneficiary, who is the first choice to receive the money, and a *contingent* beneficiary, who receives it if the primary beneficiary is no longer alive.

Some people choose to have these proceeds paid to their estates or to charitable organizations. This is something to discuss with an accountant or a lawyer when you decide to have a *will* prepared.

☑ Review any employment manuals, handbooks, or recent memoranda to employees

Frequently, one or more of these documents set forth the rights and responsibilities of employees in a company and the procedures for dealing with difficulties. It is important for a new employee to be aware of these things, so that the expected procedures can be followed. Be careful to note which individuals are designated for particular purposes. You should receive copies of these items for yourself so that they will always be available to refer to if you have any questions.

☑ Make any elections required by your retirement plan

Some retirement plans provide employees with choices as to how much of their pay will be placed in the plan. One form of retirment plan, a 401(k), provides for the employer itself to pay certain amounts of matching funds when an employee makes contributions. This plan is a very good way to defer income taxes on funds that are invested for your retirement. (Retirement plans are discussed in detail in Chapter 2.)

Some retirement plans also give employees choices with regard to how they want their retirement monies invested. Most companies that have such plans have an investment adviser who provides employees with access to someone who can make suggestions in this regard. Many employers have regular meetings with this individual, which employees are free to attend.

☑ Familiarize yourself with your rights as an employee

Every employee has certain rights. You should be aware of your rights as an employee and you should always insist upon them in a polite, but clear way. If you let your employer or someone else in connection with your job violate your rights and you do nothing about it, you are cheating yourself and perhaps others. Just as employees are obligated not to do things that hurt their employers' businesses, employers are required not to do things that hurt their employees.

Even in an employment at will, where you have no definite *term* of employment, there are two things your employer cannot use as a basis for firing or demoting you. First, your employer may not take any action against you based on your race, creed, color, religion, national origin, age, sex, sexual preference (in some states), or handicap not related to your work. This is an extremely important right and there are federal and state agencies available to help you protect it. You should always feel free to ask for their help if necessary. Very few employers today would risk the penalties involved in violations of these rights.

The second thing for which you cannot be fired or demoted regardless of your employment contract is your exercise of legally protected rights. For example, if you speak at a meeting outside of work and support a lawful organization or viewpoint that your employer does not like, you cannot be fired or disciplined for doing so. Your right of freedom of speech is protected by federal and state constitutions and you may exercise it lawfully without being penalized.

However, you must be sure that you do not exercise your rights in a way that interferes with your employer's business. For example, do not get up on a table and make a 30-minute speech in the lunchroom in support of your favorite political party every workday at noon. You have the right to say anything you want about any political party, but you do not have the right to disrupt the lunch hour of every employee at your workplace.

Employers are not entitled to interfere with your outside life when it does not interfere with your work. In general, activities like speaking at meetings outside the workplace about matters that do not concern work is beyond the reach of employers. However, an employer could legitimately be interested if, for example, it learns that an employee who operates dangerous and sensitive equipment has been arrested for the third time in six months for driving while intoxicated.

An employee is entitled to be treated respectfully, safely, and in a manner that is not personally embarrassing. Your employer may not threaten you with any form of physical action or use loud and continual brow-beating. An employer is entitled to get angry like everyone else, but that anger must be controlled and not used to inflict emotional harm on employees.

Every employee is entitled not to be subject to *sexual misconduct* by an employer or a fellow employee. Sexual misconduct in two forms is prohibited by law. The first form of sexual conduct that is prohibited is known as *quid pro quo* sexual conduct. *Quid pro quo* sexual conduct occurs when an employer or a superior at the workplace offers anything specific, like a raise or promotion, if the employee engages in some form of sexual conduct or threatens harm, such as firing or demotion, if the employee does not engage in some form of sexual conduct. There is no gray area with regard to *quid pro quo* sexual conduct. All of it is illegal, unethical, and punishable by law.

The second form of sexual misconduct at the workplace is known as *sexually-charged environment*. A sexually-charged environment is a workplace where there is too much sexual attention, even though no specific offers are made. Continual off-color jokes, repeated offensive remarks or gestures, or even inappropriate stares can create an unlawful, sexually-charged environment. With regard to this form of sexual misconduct, however, some room for judgment applies. One off-color joke that you happen not to like or an occasional offer to come to a social gathering after work would not be considered by most people to be sufficient for serious action.

Many employers have a designated individual available to receive complaints concerning sexual misconduct. If not, you should raise any such matter with your immediate superior or, if that individual is the harassor, the next highest supervisor. Sexual misconduct at the workplace is a serious matter and should not be tolerated.

 Know that every employee is entitled to work in a safe and healthy work environment

No employer has the right to ask you to do anything that is dangerous or potentially injurious to your health or welfare. If you see any such problem and it can be solved, tell your employer immediately and ask that it be solved. If the matter continues or if you become aware of something that may affect your health, but you are not sure, ask the appropriate state or federal agency responsible for occupational safety and health to assist you. The law entitles every employee to a safe and healthy environment, reasonable breaks from work, and sanitary bathroom facilities.

 Arrange to have your employer deposit your salary directly into your checking account

Picking up your paycheck, carrying it around with the possibility of losing it, and going to the bank or some other place to cash it is a waste of time. Almost every employer today—and certainly all employers with payroll services—permits employees to arrange to have their checks directly deposited into their checking accounts. Use that time for something more important than depositing your paycheck.

• • • • •

Changing Employment

When you change jobs and employers, you have two sets of matters to address—the things that are required to establish yourself with your new employer and the things that are required to leave your old employer with all of the benefits to which you are entitled. Most people do not want to spend a great deal of time on their past employment, since they are devoting themselves to establishing their new employment.

Here is a checklist of what to do when leaving an employer so you do not lose anything to which you are entitled.

Checklist for Ending Employment

- ❏ Get your final compensation
- ❏ Review your retirement plan
- ❏ Continue your medical insurance coverage
- ❏ Review your rights regarding continuance of life and disability insurance coverage
- ❏ Obtain a reference from your old employer
- ❏ Resolve any restrictive covenant matters

Get your final compensation

In addition to your customary pay for the last period you worked, you may be entitled to a *severance payment* or additional pay for accrued but unused leave time, unpaid commissions, or other things. Be sure that you agree on what you are entitled to *before* you leave your employer, since it is much more difficult to do this after you have departed.

Review your retirement plan

If you have a retirement plan with your employer and you are changing employers, there are several possibilities. At the time you complete your employment with your old employer, you must determine the extent to which you are *vested* in the money in your retirement account. If you are 100% vested, you are entitled to all of the money. If not, you are entitled to either a smaller percentage or none at all, depending upon your old employer's vesting schedule and how long you worked there. To the extent you are vested in money in your retirement account, you are entitled to it forever, regardless of whether you leave an employer. (The concept of vesting is more fully explained in Chapter 2.)

In some cases, people leave money in a retirement plan of a past employer because they have no preferable place to put it. Since people who manage retirement plans have a legal obligation to care for everyone's money in the plan, you should not have to worry that your retirement money will be taken by someone not entitled to it. The more frequent choice, however, is to put the money in the retirement plan of your past employer either into a new plan with your new employer or into an *Individual Retirement Account*—an IRA. Moving retirement monies in this fashion is known as a *rollover*, and it is a very common occurrence. Investment firms offer rollover kits and free advice about rollovers as a way of getting business.

The crucial thing to be certain of when retirement funds are moved from one retirement plan to another is that the change is accomplished in a way that does not destroy the *tax-exempt advantages* of retirement plans. If you have any doubt about this matter, check with your accountant or tax preparer.

☑ Continue your medical insurance coverage continues

If you have been a member of a medical plan through your past employer, you are almost certainly entitled to what is known as a *COBRA*. COBRA is a federal law that entitles departing employees to continue belonging to medical plans of past employers for eighteen months in normal circumstances, and twenty-nine months if you leave on account of a disability. Depending upon your new employer's medical insurance plan and your personal situation with regard to obtaining other medical insurance, you may wish to take advantage of this right.

You must provide a formal notice to your past employer that you want to exercise your COBRA right. Employers are required to provide departing employees with notice of their COBRA right and a form for exercising it. If you elect to exercise your COBRA right, you must be certain to pay the cost of your medical insurance to your past employer monthly. Some employers will bill you for such expenses. (The employer is also entitled to impose a very small handling charge for this matter.)

 Review your rights regarding continuance of life and disability insurance coverage

Unlike medical insurance, you do not have the absolute legal right to continue life and disability insurance provided by your old employer. Since these forms of insurance increase in price as you get older, and sometimes can no longer be purchased at all, you should do everything possible to continue such policies after you stop working for your old employer. Often, such policies do have guaranteed renewability provisions that extend beyond your past employment. You are always free to contact the insurance broker or agent who provided those policies to your past employer to determine what future rights you may have regarding those policies.

 Obtain a reference from your old employer

When you leave one employer and go to work for another, you should be certain to get a good letter of reference from your past employer. The letter should be from someone with reasonable authority who was familiar with your work and is willing to write a good reference letter for you.

Usually such letters are made out "To Whom It May Concern," because it is not clear at the time they are acquired who will be getting them.

If your employer is unwilling to give you a good letter, you should do your best to agree that a particular person will be available to write one if requested by another employer. It is a good idea, whether you leave with a reference letter or not, to agree upon the identity of the person who should be contacted if anyone wants a reference about you. You can usually agree with that person that he or she will be available for such a purpose and that, if called, he or she will say certain favorable things about you. It makes a very good impression on future employers that someone with knowledge and authority at a past employer has confirmed the positive things you are telling the new employer about yourself.

Resolve any restrictive covenant matters

If your contract with your old employer restricts you in some way with respect to future employment, be certain that you have addressed that matter. If you are planning to go to work for a new employer who is not affected by the restrictive covenant, you may nevertheless need to obtain a letter for the new employer stating that this is the case. New employers of persons who may have had restrictive covenants with former employers are always concerned about that matter.

If you are planning to go to work for a new employer who is covered in some way by your restrictive covenant with your old employer, you have several choices. The best choice is to convince your old employer to forego whatever rights it may have under the restrictive covenant and provide you with a letter to that effect. If this fails, you have two choices left.

One is to continue to pursue new employment even though the restrictive covenant stands in the way. This is risky business because no one knows for certain whether a past employer will try to enforce a restrictive covenant, and if it does, whether the court will uphold it. If this happens, one thing is for sure—you will bear considerable expenses and aggravate your new employer. The other possibility, and the one that is recommended, is to consult an attorney who is familiar with this area of work. If you are lucky, your new employer, with whom you should be truthful about the matter, may provide you with help from its attorney. If not, you should inquire about a competent and reasonably priced attorney. In many instances, attorneys are able to negotiate compromises so that their clients may pursue new employment.

CHAPTER 2

Managing Finances

I am not a financial advisor. Nevertheless, it would be impossible to practice law for a long time for a lot of clients without recognizing that people who get into financial trouble have usually made certain basic mistakes. Unfortunately, a lot of these people find themselves in legal difficulties that are offensive and costly. Claims of creditors and collection agencies, lawsuits, and sometimes bankruptcies occur much too often to people who could have avoided them. Frequently, once things start going wrong, they go from bad to worse. Difficulties with jobs, spouses, and children often follow financial and legal problems.

The advice in this chapter depends upon two things. First, you need a source of a reasonable amount of income to make anything work. For most, this means a job, a partner with a job, or both. Second, you must have some self-control over how you spend money. If you make a modest income and have to drive a Lexus and watch television on a 42-inch plasma screen, there is very little anyone can say to help you. However, if you have a decent income and reasonable control over your spending, there are a lot of things you can do to make things better for yourself.

Checklist for Managing Your Finances

- ❑ Establish and maintain credit
- ❑ Obtain only one credit card and use it properly
- ❑ Pay your bills promptly each month
- ❑ Do not become jointly liable for obligations unless you understand what you are doing
- ❑ Repay your student loans
- ❑ Understand the standard agreements you are making
- ❑ Write confirmatory letters about important matters
- ❑ Use your checking account carefully
- ❑ Utilize a tax-qualified retirement plan to the maximum extent possible

☑ Establish and maintain credit

Credit is your track record with regard to meeting your financial responsibilities, sometimes called your *creditworthiness*. If you pay your bills on time and no one has any lawsuits against you, your credit should be fine. But not all credit is the same. Depending upon your earnings, the property you own, and other factors, you may have credit up to a certain amount of money, but not beyond that amount. This is sometimes called your *borrowing capacity*.

In the beginning, you have no credit whatsoever. That is why the *guaranty* of a parent or other responsible person may be necessary for things such as credit cards. As time proceeds and you prove yourself worthy of the amount of credit that has been extended to you, your creditworthiness and the amount of credit you may acquire increase.

You may find it difficult to get your first credit card. However, when you do get it (and use it responsibly), you will become flooded with invitations to get other credit cards. One of the strange things about credit is that often those who need it least have the most of it. For the average person, establishing credit is a process of receiving a limited amount of credit, using it wisely, and then receiving more and more credit up to the point your circumstances justify.

There are a number of companies and services that obtain credit information and make it available for a fee. For most people, the most important credit information available to others is found in three agencies: Equifax, TransUnion, and Experian.

Addresses for Major Credit Reporting Agencies

Equifax Credit Information Services, Inc.
P.O. Box 740241
Atlanta, GA 30374
800-356-4715
www.equifax.com

TransUnion, LLC
P.O. Box 2000
Chester, PA 19022
800-888-4213
www.transunion.com

Experian
P.O. Box 2002
Allen, TX 75013
888-397-3742
www.experian.com

For a fee that is set by the federal government ($8.50 plus tax), subject to slight increases or decreases in some cases, you may obtain a copy of your credit report from any of these three agencies. Unless there is some kind of a mixup, the information on the report should be the same from all three (although how each ranks or *scores* your credit may be different). Normally, your credit information will begin to appear in these agencies after several months of financial independence. Some people like to check their credit rating once a year or so, and you certainly can too. However, if you have no reason to suspect a problem, it is not necessary to check your credit rating on a regular basis. You might want to check it before a new substantial expenditure, such as for a car or certainly for a house, when you will be borrowing money.

Problems with regard to your credit rating can be difficult to handle. If the problem is due to a mistake on the part of a business or bank, you should demand that it correct the information immediately. Do this by a letter sent by certified mail, return receipt requested. Businesses that give erroneous credit information about someone to the agencies—and refuse to correct it promptly once they are advised—are subject to penalties. Most businesses will promptly correct the error once they learn of it.

If bad information is correct, however, you better get busy curing the problem. Bad credit does go away after a period of time has passed during which you have satisfactory credit, but this does not happen immediately. If the bad information comes from a particular party to whom you owe money (a *creditor*), straighten things out with that party. Sometimes you can do this by agreeing to a payment schedule you can live with and other times you can do it by paying off the bill as soon as possible. The surest way to keep a bad credit rating is to dodge a creditor to whom you owe money. Creditors hate being avoided by customers and they take their anger out by messing up their credit.

Since credit depends upon responsibly paying bills, you will not establish any credit unless you have some bills. If you never charge anything, never use a credit card, never order anything without sending the money first, and pay all your basic bills in advance, you will never establish any credit. This is strange because if you did these things, you would probably be the most reliable debtor in the world. However, since you will want to have credit at different times in the future, you should take reasonable steps to establish it.

☑ Obtain only one credit card and use it properly

No one needs more than one credit card. Although it may take a little while, you will ultimately be able to establish a credit limit that is appropriate for you with one credit card company. People who use multiple credit cards invariably have unpaid balances at the end of each month and get into trouble. The interest rates on credit cards are absurdly high and people who maintain unpaid balances on credit cards are far and away the most likely to wind up in serious trouble.

☑ Pay your bills promptly each month

Credit card bills—like all bills—should be paid in full every month. This is an obvious item, but many people fail to observe it. Be sure that when you pay your bills you do not bounce checks. You maintain good credit by prompt payment that causes your creditors no difficulty. If you have any question about whether you are writing a check or using a credit card satisfactorily, check it out before you do so. Once creditors start putting bad information in your credit record, it is very hard to clean it up.

Do not become jointly liable for obligations unless you understand what you are doing

Your credit can be spoiled by involving yourself with someone else in the wrong way. For example, if you and a friend lease an apartment together and agree to split the rent, you will be stuck if your roommate decides to leave for another city while your lease is still ongoing. If you can afford the entire rent, your landlord will probably come after you more forcefully than your out-of-state roommate, and if you do not pay, you may wind up with a bad credit rating.

Any time you undertake a financial obligation with someone else, be sure you have made a good judgment about the other person and reach a firm understanding about who is responsible for how much of the bills. Remember that most of the time when two people undertake an obligation together, and it does not specify otherwise, the obligation is a *joint and several* obligation. Putting aside the legalese, this means that each person is liable for the entire obligation insofar as the creditor is concerned. The law usually says that if two people have an agreement between them that they will split an obligation, that agreement is their problem, but the creditor may go after either one of them for the entire amount. If your friend is out-of-state or bankrupt, this does not leave you in a very good position.

 Repay your student loans

If you are starting out on your own after completing schooling that was paid for in whole or in part by a student loan, your budget will be affected for quite a few years by your obligation to repay the loan. The largest source of student loans are the *Student Financial Assistance Programs* of the federal government. These various loans are administered by the U.S. Department of Education. In some situations, parents are the borrowers and in other situations, students are the borrowers (with or without the parents). If you have one of these loans, such as a *Stafford Loan*, a *Perkins Loan*, or any other federal loan, you should obtain the literature describing the repayment obligations.

There is a booklet called *Paying Back Your Student Loan* available from the Department of Education about this matter. (There are also some federal grants, such as *Pell Grants*, that do not require repayment. If you have one of these, be sure that you have done everything you need to do in order to be free of any repayment obligation.)

In addition to student financial assistance loans from the federal government, most states have some form of state-funded financial aid for education. These loans generally require residence in the state and attendance at a state institution, sometimes with a particular grade average being maintained. Your state Department of Education should be able to supply you with literature concerning the repayment obligations pertaining to these loans. (Some states also have scholarships that do not require repayment. If you have received one of those, be sure that you have done whatever is necessary to free you from any repayment obligation.)

In addition to federal and state loans, various banks provide what are known as *alternative loans*. These are loans to students who do not qualify for federal or state financial aid or need more money than those sources can provide. Alternative loans are not guaranteed by the federal or state governments, and therefore, interest rates and repayment terms are generally less favorable.

Student loans of all kinds require repayment to begin within a certain time after graduation. Typically, the time period is six months or one year. You will need to check regarding your particular loans to determine when repayment must begin. In most instances, the interest rate on student loans increases after graduation. Even though the interest rates on student loans are generally favorable, this is something you must take into account.

One of the things you must look at carefully if you have a student loan is the circumstances that may justify a *deferment* of your repayment obligation or even a cancellation of some or all of it. Some of these are known as *Forgiveness Programs*, since they forgive part or all of your repayment obligation if you qualify for the particular program. For example, the *Stafford Loan Forgiveness Program* for teachers provides some very favorable deferments or cancellations if you teach in low-income schools or shortage areas for a particular amount of time.

Once you have determined when you are obligated to begin repayment of your loan, how much the interest rate will be during the time you repay the loan, and whether you can qualify for any deferments or cancellations, you should be able to compute the amount of your monthly payment to repay your student loan. Be sure that you know your total balance when you begin repayment. Even though the interest rate while you are in school is generally the lowest during any portion of the time the loan is outstanding, your beginning balance may include a good deal of interest if you have been in school for a number of years.

The bank that provided the loan to you will assist you in making this determination and advise you about possible repayment alternatives. Obviously, the longer you take to repay the loan, the smaller the monthly payments will be.

☑ Understand the standard agreements you are making

Contracts for standard services, such as local and long-distance telephone services, cable television services, services related to the Internet, services for banking matters, and even utility services, differ widely. What you want, of course, is the service that is least expensive for you given the way you use that particular service. However, this is often difficult to determine since service providers are tricky. You may elect, for example, to pay a flat electric or gas charge throughout the year, without realizing that there is a catch-up provision if you exceed the predicted total cost. You may use a long-distance telephone service that has a very attractive per-minute rate, but a hookup or other charge that winds up costing you a good deal more than other services.

There is no substitute for reading the contracts you are entering and asking questions about them until you are satisfied. This process can be time-consuming and boring, but it will save you a good deal of disappointment in the end. A couple of things are particularly worth remembering.

First, there is no free lunch. If something seems too good to be true, it probably is. Second, when you get a new service, examine your bills particularly carefully for the first few months to be sure they are consistent with what you believe you agreed to. If that is not the case, take it up immediately with the service provider and do not be shy about canceling the service if it is not coming out the way you expected.

✔ Write confirmatory letters about important matters

There is nothing better than a letter to confirm something that was agreed to. If you have any doubt whether the other person is going to stick with something you discussed, take a minute or two to write a confirmatory letter.

For example, if your bank confesses to a mistake that resulted in bounced checks and promises you it will make good on them and write letters to each of the recipients, write a short letter confirming that understanding. Even though the person you have spoken with may be sincere—which, unfortunately, is not always the case—that person may be replaced by someone else in the next twenty minutes.

Use your checking account carefully

The correct use of checking accounts is a serious matter. A separate checklist for that purpose is provided on the next page.

 Utilize a tax-qualified retirement plan to the maximum extent possible

This is one of the few no-brainers any investment adviser will tell you about. Tax-qualified retirement plans permit you to avoid paying income taxes on a portion of your income, which may be invested in different ways, until you retire or become disabled and start using it. In some employment situations, the funds you use in this fashion are matched by funds paid by your employer. This is additional money that you would otherwise not receive. The various types of tax-qualified retirement plans are described later in this chapter.

• • • • •

How to Handle Your Checking Account

It is amazing how many people get into trouble with the use of their checking accounts. A checking account is simply a bank's piggy bank. You put money in it by making deposits and you take money out of it by writing checks. If you follow some simple rules, you will have no difficulty with your checking account.

Checklist of Dos and Don'ts for Checking Accounts

- ❏ Do not carry your checkbook unless you plan to use it
- ❏ Do not give anyone a blank or partially completed check
- ❏ Complete all checks in indelible ink using all available space
- ❏ Do not give checks to people to cash or deposit on a conditional basis
- ❏ Complete your check ledger each time you write a check or make a deposit
- ❏ Reconcile your monthly bank statements promptly and advise the bank immediately of any errors
- ❏ Retain deposit slips, ATM receipts, check ledgers, and check stubs until all items are reconciled

✔ Do not carry your checkbook unless you plan to use it

Lost checkbooks can be a serious problem. If you do not know you have lost your checkbook and you do not check your next bank statement in time, you may lose the right to complain about forged checks. In addition, your checkbook contains your bank account number, which is something you should definitely keep to yourself.

✔ Do not give anyone a blank or partially completed check

Your bank will hold you responsible for a check if you somehow put it in motion. If you have signed a blank check, you will have a hard time convincing your bank that it should not be paid. There have been many situations in which someone who was provided with someone else's check completed it in a manner that was not authorized. This is a legal mess for the owner of the check. Avoiding it is simple.

Complete all checks in indelible ink using all available space

The best way to avoid permitting anyone to alter one of your checks is to complete every check fully in indelible ink using all available space. If there is space left over in one of the entry places, such as where you spell out the amount for which you are writing the check, use lines or squiggles to fill up that space. Checks are frequently altered by adding words to what was already there. A check with space before either the written amount or the number amount is easy to alter.

 Do not give checks to people to cash or deposit on a conditional basis

If you write a check to someone for anything, be sure you intend for them to cash it. If there is something you want to occur before the other person can cash the check, do not give it to him or her until that has occurred. The law that applies to checks does not recognize all understandings that are intended to limit their use. If you do not want someone to cash your check until next Tuesday, the law will not hold them at fault for cashing it today. If it bounces, it is your problem.

 Complete your check ledger each time you write a check or make a deposit

The most important thing you will do to keep your checking account balance correct is add the amount of each deposit and subtract the amount of each check and any fees in your record book (*check ledger*) each time you make a deposit, write a check, pull cash from an ATM, use a debit card attached to your checking account, or are charged a fee on your monthly statement. Do not postpone doing this. People often forget to do it and, if you do, your checkbook will end up unbalanced.

Reconcile your monthly bank statements promptly and advise the bank promptly of any errors

Each month your bank will send you a record of your checking account. This is known as your *monthly statement.* The rules of the bank, as well as the law, require you to review this statement within a certain amount of time, usually less than a month, after you receive it. The monthly statement indicates deposits that were made to your checking account that month, checks that were paid or other withdrawals, and fees you were charged. Remember that you may have outstanding checks that were not paid because someone did not cash them promptly.

If you do not verify (*reconcile*) your monthly statement and report any inaccuracy to the bank within the required time, you lose the right to complain about any errors. Since you do not want to lose that right if your bank fails to record a deposit to which you are entitled or subtracts monies from your account for a check you did not write, you should check your monthly statement promptly each time you receive it. A good rule is to check each monthly statement within a week of the time it arrives. If there are any errors in it or if you do not understand something about the way your account was treated, telephone the bank and ask your questions. Most situations that arise are satisfactorily resolved very quickly.

 Retain deposit slips, ATM receipts, check ledgers, and check stubs until all items are reconciled

The individual items that confirm the checks you have written and the deposits you have made are what you need to verify that your monthly bank statement is correct. If your bank returns your checks to you, or furnishes you with photocopies of them, these should be kept for several years as proof that you paid a particular account. If you have no other records for tax purposes of payments and deposits, you should keep your check ledgers and check stubs for this purpose.

NOTE: *Be sure that payments you make using debit cards or online services, and ATM withdrawals, are deducted from your checking account balance in the same manner as checks.*

• • • • •

As you can see, staying out of legal problems regarding finances depends on using bank accounts correctly. As with credit cards, the less accounts you have, the better. One checking and one savings account are satisfactory for most people. People who move money around in order to avoid creditors or make it seem as though they have more money than is really the case, usually wind up in bad legal trouble—and sometimes criminal trouble.

However, as with everything these days, banking has its own jargon. You should understand the basic terms used in banking.

Terms Used in Banking:

- **APR (annual percentage rate).** The actual amount of interest paid per year after compounding of interest is taken into account.
- **ATM machine.** An automated teller machine that is used to withdraw money from bank accounts.
- **balance.** The amount of money available in a bank account.
- **bounced check.** A check that is returned without being cashed because there is insufficient money in the account.

- **certificate of deposit (CD) (savings certificate).** Something that is purchased at a bank for a certain sum of money that the bank keeps for an agreed period of time in return for paying an agreed amount of interest.
- **credit.** A sum of money that is added to a bank account.
- **creditor.** A person or business that is owed money.
- **debit.** A sum of money that is deducted from a bank account.
- **debit card (check card).** A card that is used to pay bills or withdraw money from a checking account.
- **debtor.** A person or business that owes money to someone else.
- **deposit.** Money that is put into a bank account.
- **direct deposit.** A deposit that is made by electronic payment.
- **fee.** The charge one must pay for a checking account.
- **interest.** The amount of money, in percentage terms, paid on deposits in a bank.
- **reconcile.** Getting the correct balance in a bank account by accounting for all deposits, withdrawals and fees.
- **signatory.** A person who is authorized to use a bank account, make withdrawals, and write checks.
- **statement.** A report sent by a bank telling you your balance and what deposits, withdrawals, and expenses were charged to the account in the past month.
- **stop order (stop payment order).** An instruction to a bank not to pay a particular check.
- **wire order (wire transfer).** A transfer of money in or out of a bank by electronic means.
- **withdrawal.** Money that is taken out of a bank account.

• • • • •

Tax-Qualified Retirement Plans

Using a *tax-qualified retirement plan* makes an awful lot of sense. These are plans that permit you to put money in them and earn profits on that money without paying taxes until you begin drawing the money out, probably many years in the future. There are very few financial planning decisions that are this easy. Tax-qualified retirement plans let you put more money into your retirement plan more quickly. There are also provisions in many plans that permit the use of retirement funds in the event of disability.

Retirement plans are quite technical and it is a good idea to review the matter with someone who can answer questions about them. Many accountants have knowledge about retirement plans and they can be particularly helpful if you establish your own plan and need to file tax and other documents.

If you work for an employer that has a tax-qualified retirement plan, you will not have any say in the provisions of that plan. If the type of plan your employer utilizes is a 401(k) plan, you will be able to decide how much money you want to put in the plan and this will determine how much *matching funds* your employer will put in for you.

Federal law that applies to tax-qualified retirement plans prohibits them from being *top-heavy*. A plan is top-heavy when the highly-paid employees of a company get too great a share of the retirement money and the lower-paid employees get too little. As an employee, you are entitled to receive your fair share of retirement monies each year. You are also entitled to periodic reports about your balance in the plan and basic literature describing the plan.

Before turning to the different types of retirement plans employers may have, you should be aware of something called the *vesting schedule*. The vesting schedule determines what percentage of your money in a retirement plan belongs to you no matter what happens. For example, if a plan's vesting schedule provides that each employee becomes vested at the rate of 20% a year, an employee who leaves the company after three years will receive 60% of his or her balance in the plan. Employers use vesting schedules as a way to encourage employees to remain with the company.

Types of Retirement Plans

- Simplified Employer Pension plan (SEP)
- Simple plan
- 401(k) plan
- Defined Benefit plan
- Money Purchase Pension plan
- Profit-Sharing plan
- Individual Retirement Account (IRA)

There are six basic types of tax-qualified retirement plans used by employers and one type of plan in particular used only by individuals.

A *Simplified Employer Pension* plan (SEP) permits the employer to contribute up to 15% of each eligible employee's compensation. Employees who are in this type of plan may also contribute to an IRA.

A *Simple* plan permits employees to make salary-deferred contributions up to $6,000. Employers must make contributions to each employee as well.

A *401(k)* plan allows employees to contribute a portion of their salaries before taxes to the plan. (Employees must also do this in a SEP or Simple plan.) The maximum allowable contribution changes each year. In 2004 the amount is $10,500. Employers match employees' contributions in accordance with a formula established by the plan up to a certain amount.

A *Defined Benefit* plan is a nightmare for most employers, but if your employer has it, that is not your problem. In this type of plan, the employer sets a retirement benefit for each employee based on a percentage of that employee's compensation. The employer contributes to this plan in an amount determined by an *actuary*, so that each employee will receive the benefit amount at the time of his or her retirement. These plans often run into trouble because of the hiring of older employees, changes in investment assumptions, or underfunding of the necessary amounts of money.

A *Money Purchase Pension* plan is one in which the employer is required to make an annual contribution of up to 25% of each employee's compensation. There is presently a limit of $35,000 per employee per year.

A *Profit-Sharing* plan is a plan in which the employer makes a variable contribution of up to 15% of the total amount of compensation of all employees in the plan. A Profit-Sharing plan's contribution may be allocated to people in the plan in several ways. The formula that is used is set forth when it is established and the present limit per employee is $35,000.

An *Individual Retirement Account* (IRA) is a tax-qualified account that an individual maintains for him- or herself. If your employer provides no tax-qualified retirement plan for you or provides a plan that allows you to have your own plan as well, you can establish an IRA. An IRA permits people who are earning money to contribute up to $2,000 per year to the plan. IRA contributions are tax deductible if you (and your spouse, if you are married and have a joint IRA plan) do not participate in any other tax-qualified plan. If you do participate in another tax-qualified retirement plan, you will have to check with an accountant to determine whether your contribution is tax-deductible.

In a *Roth IRA* you pay the required taxes before you reach retirement age, so when you withdraw the funds they are tax-exempt.

There are income restrictions on Roth IRAs and restrictions about using them in connection with other retirement plans. If you wish to consider a Roth IRA, discuss the plan with an expert. Whether a Roth IRA is preferable for you depends upon things like the length of time your plan exists, your age, and your tax bracket (now and in the future). This is not an easy decision to make and you should get help in making it.

If you work for your own business and want to establish a retirement plan for it, there are many things to consider. Depending on how many employees your business has, your tax situation, your plans for retirement, and other factors, the type of plan that is best for you must be carefully considered. If you have to face this issue, use one of the professional people who establishes tax-qualified retirement plans for businesses and helps them administer those plans. There is a good deal of paperwork involved in establishing a tax-qualified retirement plan and there are tax forms that must be filed every year. The IRS is finicky about these plans if they are not correctly prepared and administered. One of your objectives should be to establish the simplest kind of plan that will satisfy your needs.

It is usually possible to change plans without losing the tax-exemption that is so valuable. (This is called a *rollover*.) Changes of employment and other circumstances may make a rollover desirable for you. Many investment companies and some banks provide rollover information as a way of getting business. Some even provide *rollover kits* containing the necessary information and documents to accomplish a rollover. The important thing is to take your time and make good decisions about retirement plans whenever you have choices to make. Retirement plans are with you for a long time and can be very important down the line.

• • • • •

Things to Do to Provide for Possible Death or Disability

If you are like most, this is not a subject you want to spend too much time on. Everyone will die someday and many people become totally or partially disabled during their lifetimes. A lot of people want to provide for these possibilities as easily and inexpensively as possible so that they can then go on with their lives. The following checklist is sufficient for nearly everybody except people with extremely complicated responsibilities and people who have so much money that ordinary preparations will not do the job. Although you can purchase forms for these purposes in legal supply stores and there are books available about drafting these documents, most people find it convenient to consult a reasonably priced, efficient lawyer about all of these matters at once. Preparing these documents is time-consuming. Even if you study the matter carefully, there are many possible errors and oversights that are easy to make.

Checklist of Things to Do to Provide for Possible Death or Disability

- ❏ Make a will
- ❏ Make a living will
- ❏ Make a durable power of attorney
- ❏ Verify beneficiaries of life insurance policies
- ❏ Designate contingent beneficiaries
- ❏ Make a folder of all documents that will be important if you die or become disabled

 **Make a will**

The reason for making a *will* (generally known as a *last will and testament*) is simple—to give you as much freedom as the law allows to decide who you want to receive the things you own after your death. If you do not have a will, a law in your state—known as the *statute of intestate succession*—will determine who receives your money and property. This may not be what you want to happen. If you are married or have children, the laws in every state restrict your freedom to give all of what you own to anyone you choose.

A will also allows you to choose the individual who will represent your estate when you die and get things handled so that what you own goes where you want it to go. This person is known as a *personal representative*. Wills also let you choose trustees for certain purposes and appoint guardians for children you are responsible for.

When you have accumulated a reasonable amount of property and money, have gotten married, and certainly when you have children—the time has come to make your first will. You can do this by yourself, if you are very careful to get the necessary information. Since the laws of each state are very specific about how wills are to be prepared and executed in order to be valid, and since there are legal possibilities regarding wills that are not obvious to most people, it is not always the best idea to prepare your own will.

A simple will is not an expensive proposition with a lawyer and using one will assure you that your will accomplishes what you want it to accomplish. In addition, a lawyer will help you deal with matters like jointly owned property, life insurance, and special needs that you may want to address. As with any such choice, make careful inquiries to get a lawyer who is competent and reasonably priced. In most states, one of the bar associations operates a lawyer referral service that can give you the names of lawyers who do simple wills in your area.

☑ Make a living will

A *living will*, which is sometimes known as an *advance directive*, tells what you want to happen if you have a very serious illness or injury. Many people do not want to receive heroic treatments or be kept alive as long as possible when there is no reasonable chance for recovery. A living will can be used to express that desire.

If you do not have a living will, decisions about such medical care will usually be made by the attending doctor in consultation with the closest relatives available. A decision made for you by other people might not reflect your wishes. For example, you may or may not want to be kept alive by certain extraordinary means, but the people who would make the decision in your absence might not be familiar with your wishes.

NOTE: *If you want to donate your organs at the time of your death, you must follow the specific procedure in your state. Contact your Department of Motor Vehicles, as in many states, this agency handles the procedures for organ donation, since many accidental deaths occur on the roads.*

It is a good idea to give a copy of your living will or any document donating your organs to your primary physician. Your doctor will generally be contacted if you are seriously ill or injured.

Make a durable power of attorney

A *durable power of attorney* is a document giving authority over your affairs to another person in the event you become too ill or incompetent to manage your affairs. The reason that the durable power of attorney is called *durable* is that it continues to exist and to give authority to another person while you are disabled from acting yourself. The other person, sometimes known as the *holder* of the durable power of attorney, acts for you if such circumstances arise, paying your bills, receiving your pay and other money, and handling your other business affairs. When you choose a personal representative for your will and a holder for your durable power of attorney, think carefully and choose an individual who is competent, trustworthy, and has the time and interest to help you.

☑ Verify beneficiaries of life insurance policies

If you have life insurance policies, they will be payable on your death to the designated beneficiaries. Sometimes the beneficiary of a life insurance policy is a person and sometimes it is the insured person's estate. Your accountant is a good person to ask about this matter, since there may be tax consequences to your choices. You can also ask a lawyer about it when you hire one to make a will for you.

☑ Be sure that you have designated contingent beneficiaries

Various sources of money that you receive will go to another person when you die. For example, monies that come to you from any form of retirement plan and also from Social Security will in most instances be paid to beneficiaries. You must be sure that you have designated the beneficiary or beneficiaries you wish to receive such monies from each source. Since it is possible that your chosen beneficiaries will not be alive at such time, you must also choose contingent beneficiaries, who will receive such monies if the beneficiaries are not available. (Some of these designations must be completed with the correct person at your employer.)

☑ Make a folder of all documents that will be important if you die or become disabled

A folder of all the documents that someone else would need in the event of your death or if you become disabled should be in a place where someone who is going to be very much involved in your affairs at such time will be able to get it. It is a good idea to tell one or more responsible people, such as a lawyer, accountant, or your personal representative, where to find this folder. Obviously, the folder should be kept either in a safe deposit box or in some secure, fireproof location over which you have control. It is very useful to include in this folder a general list of all your financial assets, such as bank accounts, stocks, bonds, mutual funds, insurance policies, and so forth. Include precise designations of these items including account numbers. This will make it a lot easier for whoever takes responsibility for your affairs to gather all the necessary knowledge efficiently.

CHAPTER 3

Your Income Taxes

Income taxes are taxes everyone must pay based upon the income each person earns. Everyone has to pay federal income tax, and most states have one as well. In a few large cities there is also a local income tax.

Terms Used in Income Tax Matters

- **audit.** A review of your income tax status by the IRS or a state taxing authority.
- **deduction.** Items that you are entitled to subtract from your income for tax purposes.
- **dependent.** A person, including yourself, for whom you provide the majority of support during a taxable year.
- **dependent exemption.** A reduction of your overall income tax for each person, including yourself, that you support.
- **enrolled agent.** A person recognized by the IRS as competent to prepare tax returns.
- **exemption.** Income that is excluded from income tax.
- **extension.** An additional amount of time permitted for filing tax returns.
- **FICA.** Federal Insurance Contributions Act consisting of Social Security and Medicare.

- **Form 1040.** The basic form for filing a federal income tax return.
- **Form 1040A.** A short form of Form 1040 many people can use in simple situations.
- **Form 1040EZ.** A short form of Form 1040 that single or married people with no dependants can use in simple situations if they meet certain other criteria.
- **Form 1099.** A form provided to you by someone for whom you did work as an independent contractor and received payment.
- **Form W-2.** A form provided to you by your employer showing your income and withholdings for the past year.
- **graduated taxes.** Taxes that increase the percentage of your income tax as it grows larger.
- **income taxes.** Taxes that are imposed on the income you earn.
- **Internal Revenue Service (IRS).** The federal agency responsible for federal tax matters.
- **Medicare.** Medical benefits to which you are entitled at retirement or disability.
- **Medicare Supplement Insurance.** An insurance policy that pays medical benefits in addition to Medicare.
- **point.** An amount of credit you receive from the FICA system based upon the FICA you have paid in past years.
- **refund.** Money that you will receive from the federal or state government because you have overpaid taxes.
- **Social Security.** Payments from the government to which you are entitled at retirement age or disability in the event you have acquired sufficient points.

- **standard deduction.** A deduction the tax laws allow you to take in lieu of specifically itemizing your deductions.
- **taxable income.** Income that is subject to income tax.
- **tax bracket.** The percentage of your income that you must pay as income taxes.
- **tax credit.** Items that reduce the actual income taxes you are required to pay.
- **tax filing deadline.** April 15th of each year, unless you receive an extension.
- **tax identification number.** A number assigned by the federal government to every taxpayer (for individuals it is their Social Security number).
- **tax preparer.** A person who prepares your tax returns for you.
- **tax return.** The forms required by federal and state government for reporting income tax obligations.
- **withholding.** Money for federal and state taxes and Social Security and Medicare that your employer deducts from your paycheck and pays to the government periodically.

The first rule about income taxes is that you must file tax returns every year by April 15th, except in unusual circumstances. You must report all of your income on those tax returns. If you have full-time employment, your employer is required to deduct certain amounts of federal and state income taxes from your salary and send that money to the federal and state governments on a very strict time schedule.

If you are self-employed or work for a business that you own and operate, you must take care of the matter of sending in taxes periodically (usually quarterly) yourself. These payments are known as *withholding* and nearly all income received by anyone requires them to be made.

At the end of each year, the whole matter comes to a head when you or your accountant (or other tax preparer) determines exactly how much income tax you owe. You are required to file your tax returns by April 15th and pay any balance that remains, or if you are lucky and have planned well, get a refund. In general, tax laws require that your withholding be at least 90% of your total tax obligation. You can be required to pay interest and penalties if this does not occur.

Each taxpayer is entitled to what is known as an *exemption* for each person he or she supports. If you support yourself and no one else, you are entitled to one exemption. As a general rule, a taxpayer may claim an exemption for another person if he or she pays more than one-half of the support of that other person. There may sometimes be a choice as to who claims someone as an exemption. This is a situation in which the advice of a good accountant or other tax preparer is needed.

The tax laws also entitle you to subtract certain expenses from your income each year. These are known as *deductions*. Deductions may be taken either by carefully itemizing them with appropriate documents such as receipts or by taking a *standard deduction*, which requires no itemization. In a few circumstances, the tax laws entitle you to deduct certain amounts from the taxes themselves. These are known as *tax credits*. You obviously want to get all of the deductions and any credits to which you are entitled. There are various free booklets available from the IRS to help you do this, but the advice of a good accountant or other tax preparer is the best way.

Free Publications from the IRS

- Publication 463—Travel, Entertainment, Gift, and Car Expenses
- Publication 334—Tax Guide for Small Businesses
- Publication 505—Tax Withholding and Estimated Tax
- Publication 525—Taxable and Non-Taxable Income
- Publication 533—Self-Employment Tax
- Publication 535—Business Expenses
- Publication 583—Starting a Business and Keeping Records
- Publication 946—How to Depreciate Property
- Publication 910—Guide to Free Tax Services

A complete listing of the booklets available from the IRS and the content of the booklets themselves may be found on the Internet at **www.irs.gov**.

Income taxes in the United States are *graduated*. This means that the percentage of your income you pay in taxes increases as your income grows larger, up to a certain point. When someone talks about their *tax bracket*, they are talking about the percentage of their income they must pay for income taxes. There are tables available that show you how much income tax you will have to pay if you earn different incomes. (The IRS has a service available to help you with these matters.) From the following tables, you can get a general idea of the amount of income tax the federal government charges taxpayers on different incomes. As you can see, the tax rates differ for single individuals, married individuals filing jointly, or surviving spouses.

Federal Tax Rates:

Single Individuals—2004

Income	Pay	+ % of	Amount
<$2,650	$0.00	0%	$0.00
<$9,700	$0.00	10%	$2,650
<$30,800	$705.00	15%	$9,700
<$68,500	$3,870.00	25%	$30,800
<$148,700	$13,295.00	28%	$68,500
<$321,200	$35,751.00	33%	$148,700
>$321,200	$92,676.00	35%	$321,200

Married Individuals Filing Jointly and Surviving Spouses—2004

Income	Pay	+ % of	Amount
<$8,000	$0.00	0%	$0.00
<$22,300	$0.00	10%	$8,000
<$64,750	$1,430.00	15%	$22,300
<$118,050	$7,797.50	25%	$64,750
<$185,550	$21,122.50	28%	$118,050
<$326,100	$40,022.50	33%	$185,550
>$326,100	$86,404.00	35%	$326,100

You should be aware that income taxes are charged on what is known as *taxable income*. Taxable income is less than total income, since it takes into account certain adjustments, deductions, and exemptions.

• • • • •

FICA (Social Security and Medicare)

In addition to income taxes, the law requires you to pay what is known as FICA based upon your earnings. FICA stands for *Federal Insurance Contributions Act* and includes Social Security and Medicare. If you are employed by someone else, your employer is required to deduct FICA from each of your paychecks according to a formula. For Social Security, the deduction is currently 6.2% of your income up to $84,900 per year. If you earn more than this amount, you are not required to pay additional Social Security. Medicare currently requires a deduction of 1.45% per year on your entire earnings.

Your employer is required to match both your Social Security and Medicare payments. Since Social Security and Medicare are an important part of the retirement plan for nearly everyone, you want to be certain that these deductions are taken from your pay properly and turned over to the tax authorities. If you are self-employed, you will be responsible for taking care of this matter yourself.

The Social Security system is based on points. You need a total of 40 points to qualify for full Social Security when you reach the required age or earlier if you become disabled. If you are starting full-time employment at a reasonably young age, say in your early 20's and intend to work until sometime in your 60's, you do not need to worry about the formula. You will easily earn the required points to be fully qualified before the time for payments arrives. You will also be fully entitled to Medicare payments, so you do not need to worry about that matter either.

If you begin work later in life, say your 40's or 50's, you should be aware that in order to receive full Social Security benefits it will take you ten years of full-time work to earn your 40 points. For people born after 1929, the general requirement is that they have worked for forty quarters as full-time employees. There are a few forms of work, notably in the public sector, that do not count for this purpose. The requirements for Medicare are slightly different, but can generally be satisfied within the same time period. Medicare benefits may be obtained before retirement age in the event of certain disabilities. Survivors of recipients of Social Security are sometimes entitled to receive certain benefits as well.

You should know that the part of Medicare that pays hospital bills (Part A) does not require you to pay any additional money to receive coverage once you reach the required age. The part of Medicare that pays doctors (Part B), however, requires you to pay a fee every month. At present, that amount is $66.60. It may be too early for you to be thinking about this matter seriously, but you should know in the back of your mind that when you reach retirement age you will probably be paying for Part B of Medicare as well as paying what is known as a Medicare supplement health insurance policy. In the meantime, do not worry about Social Security and Medicare as long as you are employed and you are or your employer is paying the required amounts for them.

• • • • •

W-2s and 1099s

There are two forms for reporting your income that you should know about. *W-2 forms* are forms prepared by employers showing the earnings of employees and the federal tax, state tax, and FICA taxes withheld from those earnings. Sometimes, W-2s show other deductions from your paycheck as well, but taxes and FICA are the required ones.

A *1099 form* is one that says that someone paid money to you for some purpose. This form is usually provided when a business makes payments for services to nonemployees on a regular basis. For example, if you occasionally write an article in the newspaper, but are not its employee, you will receive a 1099 form before tax time indicating that you were paid whatever amount you received.

You are obligated to report all the income you receive whether you get W-2 or 1099 forms or not. Copies of W-2 and 1099 forms go to the taxing authorities. If you fail to report income that was stated on one of these forms, sooner or later you will receive a letter from the IRS advising you to straighten the matter out.

This is the type of form your employer is required to give you every year before January 31st. You or your accountant or tax preparer use this form to prepare your tax returns and provide copies of it with your tax returns.

62 Starting Out or Starting Over

This form is used to report income to you as an independent contractor. It is also used by you or your accountant or tax preparer to prepare your tax returns, but you do not need to provide copies of it with your tax returns, unless there has been withholding shown on the Form 1099. For example, if a bank sends a Form 1099-INT for bank interest and has withheld federal income tax, the Form 1099 should be provided with the tax return to show that federal taxes were withheld.

W-2s and 1099s are supposed to be sent to everyone by January 31st of each year. Invariably, these forms are provided late. There is no real problem about this as long as you get your forms in time to provide them to the accountant or tax preparer who will be preparing your tax returns. You should receive a form reflecting interest or other income from every bank, insurance company, or investment firm from which you received income in the taxable year. If you are preparing your own tax returns, you must be sure to receive the forms in time to get your tax returns filed by April 15th.

Be sure to keep these forms in a folder in your record box so that they will be available for preparation of your tax returns. Be sure when you receive these forms that you look them over carefully to be certain that the information provided is correct. Since some employers prepare a lot of these forms, it is possible that your income or taxes withheld could be confused with someone else's. You know how much money is being taken out of your paycheck for taxes and FICA each time you are paid and, therefore, you should be able to compute the total amounts for the entire year.

• • • • •

Filing Tax Returns

Filing tax returns is one of those jobs everyone would like to avoid. Whether you prepare your own returns or someone else does it, you will have to review what you did financially for the entire year to be certain that you report each required item correctly and receive all deductions to which you are entitled. Once you have done this once or twice, the process becomes easier. However, you need to have a system for doing it to make it work correctly.

The best system for you to use is this. Before you start adding things up and going through your checks and bills, determine precisely what information you need. For example, if you are paying a significant amount of money for uninsured medical expenses, you will want to know the total amount to see if it is large enough to entitle you to a tax deduction. If you are paying automobile expenses for your work and not being reimbursed by your employer, you will want to know this total amount. If you buy a house, you will want to know the total amount of interest you are paying on your mortgage so that you can receive a tax deduction for it. Your accountant or tax preparer will help you think of all the information you need for your tax returns.

Once you have determined all the categories of information you need and have written them down, you are ready to begin the really boring part of the work. The really boring part is going through every check you have written for the entire year (or all of your check stubs if your cancelled checks are not returned to you by the bank), every bill you have paid, and all the money you have received during the year. Do not forget to include cash expenses that fall under one of the categories if you have receipts for them. Do not forget to include in your income any interest you have received from bank accounts. Do not forget to figure out expenses that cannot be determined simply by looking at one check or bill. For example, if you are entitled to a home office deduction, you will need to determine all of your house or apartment expenses and the percentage of your home's area that is devoted exclusively to your office. Whether you use an accountant or tax preparer or do the returns yourself, it is useful to make a worksheet for any items like these that need to be calculated.

Checklist for Preparing for Tax Time

❏ Select an accountant or other tax preparer
❏ Be certain that you have no deductions or other items that could benefit you on the long form if you plan to use Form 1040A or Form 1040EZ for your federal tax return
❏ Gather all of your W-2s and 1099s for the entire year
❏ Review all the records you have kept for the taxable year, including all of your checks or check stubs
❏ Get all materials to your accountant or other tax preparer well in advance of April 15th of each year
❏ Review and sign your tax returns once they are ready
❏ File your tax returns and pay any balance that is owed

☑ Select an accountant or other tax preparer

Unless your life is extremely simple or you have a lot of tax knowledge, do not prepare your own tax returns. An accountant or other tax preparer will not only make the job much easier for you (at what should be a relatively low cost), but will also be able to find deductions or other items for you that will justify the fee. It is also very useful to have such an individual available to you for questions from time to time. Selecting and using an accountant or tax preparer is a subject worth a separate discussion. (You will find this information in the next section of this chapter.)

A number of tax preparation programs for use on a computer are available today. One of the most popular is *Turbo Tax*. For people who do not want to utilize a tax preparer, these programs are very useful. However, if you are inclined to do your own tax returns in this manner, know that there may be things potentially beneficial to your tax situation that the computerized program will not uncover.

Be certain that you have no deductions or other items that could benefit you on the long form if you plan to use Form 1040A or Form 1040EZ for your federal tax return

For the simplest of tax situations, there are very brief federal forms known as *short form 1040s*. Form 1040A is available for many people to use in simple situations. Form 1040EZ is available for use by single or married people with no dependants in simple situations, meeting certain criteria. You will find these criteria on the IRS website at **www.irs.gov.** These forms do not make it possible for you to take itemized deductions or other adjustments that may be of benefit to you. If you have such items in your tax situation, you should not use these forms.

 Gather all of your W-2s and 1099s for the entire year

You must report all of your income, whether or not it is reflected on a W-2 or a 1099. Most people receive these forms each taxable year with no problems. W-2s must be included with your federal and state tax returns. Banks and other places where you receive interest, dividends, or other forms of income are required to send you a 1099 form after the end of each year. Generally, 1099 forms do not need to be sent in with your tax return.

 Review all the records you have kept for the taxable year, including all of your checks or check stubs

Your review of these materials should be as complete as possible, since there may be items that entitle you to a deduction or tax credit that you have not been thinking about. For example, if you purchased work supplies or used a home office, total each category of expenditure for such purposes. If you use an accountant or other tax preparer, he or she will be of help to you in explaining the categories of items to be assembled.

☑ Get all materials to your accountant or other tax preparer well in advance of April 15th of each year

People who prepare tax returns are awfully busy in the weeks just preceding April 15th. It is a very good idea to get all of your materials to such people well in advance of that date. Tax preparers have more time to review your materials carefully and obtain the maximum benefit if you do not deliver them at the last minute. If you wind up using the same person or firm regularly, you can agree on a date by which you will furnish all of your materials.

Also, when you deliver your materials, have them as organized as possible. A simple sheet of paper providing a total for things, such as gas receipts for a business vehicle or miscellaneous office supplies, is very useful. Paperclip the identifying slip of paper to the full stack of receipts so that your tax preparer will not have to search around for such items. Do not forget to include checks and receipts for all tax-exempt contributions. Your accountant or other tax preparer should return all of these materials to you with your finished tax returns.

☑ Review and sign your tax returns once they are ready

When you get ready to sign your tax returns, review them carefully. If they were prepared by a tax preparer, they will usually be given to you with precise instructions about signing them. Bear in mind that these documents are considered to be under oath and must be free of any intentional false statements.

☑ File your tax returns and pay any balance that is owed

Unless you are applying for an extension, you must file your tax returns before the end of the day, April 15th. If you are unable for any reason to do this, the IRS and your state tax agency will provide you with appropriate forms for seeking an *extension*. If you use a tax preparer, he or she can do this as well. If you are unable to pay a balance that is owed, you may defer your payment by following procedures the IRS, your state tax office, or your tax preparer will explain. This does not, however, excuse you from filing your tax returns on time. Be certain when you file your returns that you retain copies of them, including W-2s, 1099s, and any other documents that are being filed with them.

Every taxpayer's situation is different and has its own wrinkles, but one rule applies to everyone. *Report all of your income to the IRS and state taxing authorities!* Some people who earn their income in ways that do not result in information going to the taxing authorities, such as those who get small fees or are paid in cash, believe they can skim some of that income and not report it at all. Some of these people are so cocky about this that they even tell customers that they want to be paid *under the table*. This is a crime, and although some people get away with it, there are a lot of people in this country who have been shocked to learn that the taxing authorities found out what they were doing and arrested them. It is not a crime to pay your honestly reported taxes late and it is not a crime to claim a deduction that the government disagrees with you about, but it is a very serious crime to say anything that is false on a tax return, and the most serious falsehood is lying about your income.

• • • • •

Selecting and Using an Accountant or Other Tax Preparer

Even when you are making a small income, a good accountant or other tax preparer, who is reasonably priced and available to you when you need advice, is a very useful person to get to know. An accountant or other tax preparer that is right for you should be able to do a number of things. He or she should be able to tell you everything you need to know about your income taxes and prepare your federal and state tax returns once a year when you need them. He or she should be able to give you advice about retirement plans and how to get the necessary paperwork done quickly and inexpensively. He or she should be able to prepare the necessary tax returns if you have your own retirement plan. If you are self-employed or have a small business that employs you, he or she should be able to help you with the necessary payroll matters and with things such as workers' compensation and unemployment insurance.

A good accountant will also make suggestions to you for saving money on your taxes and will help you implement those suggestions. For example, if you are self-employed, a good accountant will help you use a home office deduction. If you have work-related expenses that entitle you to tax deductions, a good accountant will review those matters with you.

NOTE: *It is recommended that most people establish and maintain a relationship with an accountant when they begin full time employment. This recommendation is not made with regard to lawyers. You may need a lawyer for special circumstances, but you do not need a lawyer on an ongoing basis like an accountant.*

Generally, accountants have the knowledge you need for your regular tax and business affairs. There are also tax preparers, some of whom are known as *enrolled agents* (EAs) and recognized by the IRS, that can do these things as well. In either event, your choice of the right person is very important. Ask your friends and business associates for recommendations. When you have a few good ones, prepare a list of questions to ask each individual. Do not be shy about asking questions about fees, availability, and experience.

Do not shoot too high or too low. You do not want to pay for an accountant in a fancy downtown office. On the other hand, you do not want to use someone who does not practice regularly and does not have an established clientele. In general, small firms of two to ten accountants are able to handle the affairs of most people quite effectively. Be sure to meet the person you are planning on using before you start working with him or her.

There are two particular ways of dealing with an accountant that will save you a lot of time and money. The first is to schedule one meeting a year and to come to that meeting fully prepared for it. A good time for the meeting is either a few weeks before the end of each year or a month or so before the tax filing deadline of April 15th. Prepare your questions in advance of the meeting and organize any documents you need to discuss before you go.

Most accountants and other tax preparers today use a form for obtaining the information they need to prepare tax returns. Review that form before your meeting and make notes of any questions you have regarding it. If you have questions about what you should be doing in the forthcoming year, schedule the meeting before the end of the year so that you can get answers before the new year begins. You should begin each year with a system in place for doing all the things and keeping all the records necessary to accomplish what you discuss with your accountant.

Do not be one of those people who puts all sorts of stuff in a bag or box and gives it to your accountant to sort out and organize. If you do this, you will pay for it. If you keep your records in separate folders in a record box from the beginning of the year until the end, everything you need for your meeting with your accountant and for the preparation of your tax returns will be easily available. When you need totals of things, such as office expenses, gas, or uninsured medical expenses, make the totals yourself before going to the meeting.

(You can use a calculator as well as your accountant and you do not need to pay for the time it will take him or her to do it.)

The second way to save cost and time concerns how you ask questions that arise periodically and how your accountant answers them. The method you should agree upon is one whereby you can send a fax or email to your accountant with the understanding that he or she will answer it in the same fashion and you will not speak with one another unless it is absolutely necessary.

For example, if you are a stone mason and your portable generator broke down in early December, you may want to ask your accountant whether you should replace it this year or in a few weeks (after the new year). There are tax laws that provide a much more favorable tax deduction for certain purchases up to certain amounts in each year. Your accountant can tell you instantly whether you have used up the favorable deduction for the current year or whether it makes no difference when you buy the new generator. If you have an accountant who is familiar with your situation and has prepared your tax returns in past years, he or she will be able to answer this sort of question immediately and the less time he or she spends, the smaller your bill. This is one reason why a regular accountant provides better service at a lower price.

> *A sample fax and a sample email with responses follow. They demonstrate some of the types of questions you may have for your accountant and what a response may contain.*

Sample Fax to an Accountant

VIA FACSIMILE
DATE: December 8, 2004
TO: Edith Silvers, C.P.A.
FROM: John McCauley

Edith,
My portable generator just blew up for the last time. I absolutely need to replace it as soon as possible and it will run about $6,800. Any advice?
John

Sample Response Fax from an Accountant

12/9/04

John,
There is a tax law allowing you to deduct certain equipment costs as an expense instead of depreciating them over a number of years. In the case of your $6,800 new generator, using this tax law will save you close to $2,000 in taxes. However, you have used up your allotment for 2004. Therefore, buy the new generator as soon as possible after the new year and you will get the tax savings.

   I hope you can hold out until then.

Happy Holidays! Edith

Sample Email to an Accountant

To: esilvers@silvercpas.com
From: mwiggins@wigginsmail.com
Date: January 23, 2005
Re: Accounting Question

Edith,
Joe wants to go to a sales convention in the Virgin Islands that is coming up next month. His employer will pay for $1,000 of the cost since this is how much allowance Joe gets for this each year in his contract. We figure the cost for both of us with airfare, hotel, etc. will run close to $2,000. Do we get a tax deduction for the part we pay?
Mary

Sample Response Email from an Accountant

To: mwiggins@wigginsmail.com
From: esilvers@silvercpas.com
Date: January 24, 2005
Re: Accounting Question

Mary,
If the trip is for business and it serves a business purpose for spouses to be present, you and Joe can deduct the cost of the trip minus the amount Joe's employer pays. Obviously, if you rack up any expenses that are not part of the business purpose, you cannot deduct those.
   Don't forget to take your bathing suits!
Edith

Edith Silvers, C.P.A.
Silver CPAs, Inc.

A good accountant will be aggressive about getting you all the tax benefits to which you are entitled, but not so aggressive that you are placed in risky situations. Make it clear to your accountant that this is precisely what you want him or her to do. Do not push your accountant to take deductions he or she does not feel you are honestly entitled to. Do not push your accountant to make representations about things that he or she is not comfortable making. If your accountant is simply too timid for your liking, get a new accountant. Your relationship with your accountant is for the long term. Long term relationships do not work well if someone is doing things that are not comfortable for both parties.

• • • • •

Dealing with the IRS and State Taxing Authorities

Although you have probably heard horror stories about letters or phone calls from the IRS or your state tax office, most of the time the people you wind up dealing with in tax matters are quite reasonable. Assuming you are an honest taxpayer doing your best to file correct tax returns, there are a few simple rules for dealing with taxing authorities.

Most dealings with taxing authorities begin with some form of written communication coming to you. The communication may be an ordinary letter or some sort of form or notice. It usually tells you exactly what you are required to do. For example, people sometimes forget to report interest received on a bank account they rarely use. Even though each bank is required to send you an interest statement each year for tax purposes, once in a while something goes wrong.

In this event, you will probably receive a letter from the IRS advising you that you have omitted the income. This type of letter may arrive many months after your tax return is filed. If the IRS is correct, you simply pay the tax that is owed and the matter is ended. Do this exactly the way the letter tells you to so that it will be recorded properly. In most circumstances, it is not necessary for an amended tax return to be prepared.

If a taxing authority sends you a letter disputing something you have claimed on your tax return—perhaps a deduction the government does not feel you are entitled to take—you have two choices. One is to concede the matter and pay the tax that is owed. The other is to dispute the matter using the procedure the taxing authority has explained in its communication. If you used an accountant or other tax preparer, that person should be advised immediately of any such matter and his or her assistance requested.

Accountants and tax preparers will attend any necessary meetings in these matters and, since you have followed the advice you were given, you definitely want your accountant to be present. As a general rule, you should only fight the battles that are worth fighting. Do not go to the mat with hearings and appeals for a $50 item. The first rule in any dispute is to get it over with.

Since most states follow federal law with regard to the majority of tax matters, the IRS is almost always the leader in raising a matter. Do not forget that if something has to be corrected with regard to your federal taxes, the chances are it also has to be corrected for your state taxes. Once you have agreed with the IRS about how a matter will be corrected, it is easy to correct it with the state taxing authorities as well. Do not be shy about asking questions of tax authorities so that you can get a matter corrected and get on with more important things.

If you give reasonable and prompt attention to matters tax authorities raise and do what they indicate is necessary to get them resolved, you should have no difficulties with your taxes. Although any notice from the IRS is always a little intimidating, a lot of matters are set straight with a brief letter or copies of one or two documents. Whatever you send to the taxing authorities, be sure to keep copies in your tax folder so that you will have them available for future reference.

Section II

The Necessities

Home and Car

CHAPTER 4

Renting an Apartment

Renting an apartment, like many jobs you need to do, begins with clarifying your intentions and ends with being certain that the documents you sign and other steps you take will get you where you want to go. In this case, you already have an idea about what sort of apartment you would like to rent. You do not need anyone's help to decide what sort of neighborhood you would like to live in, what features you would like your apartment to have, and how much you are willing to pay. In a perfect world, you could get everything you want in an apartment at a price you are willing to pay. Since this is not a perfect world, your job is to take steps that will get you as much of what you want as possible and will assure that you satisfactorily address all the essential matters.

Finding an Apartment

The first thing you must do to rent a satisfactory apartment is find one. Some people do this easily through friends or acquaintances, but sometimes the process is somewhat difficult and time consuming. Even if you quickly identify an apartment that seems to be suitable for you, there are certain steps you should take before renting it to be sure you will be satisfied once you have signed the lease. Follow all the steps recommended on the following checklist, even if they do not seem at first to be necessary. If you do, you will not experience disappointments about your apartment after it is too late to do anything about them.

Checklist for Finding an Apartment

- ❏ Determine the essentials of a satisfactory apartment
- ❏ Define the geographic area that would be acceptable to you
- ❏ Walk around the area you are considering and read signs and newspaper ads about apartments in it
- ❏ Decide whether to use a real estate broker
- ❏ Check out everything in an apartment that interests you
- ❏ Obtain a copy of the lease

✔ Determine the essentials of a satisfactory apartment

The essentials of a satisfactory apartment are the *must have* items. If you cannot live without air conditioning, put it on your list. If you need to have easy access to public transportation or a parking place for your car, put it on your list. If you have a pet, be sure that pets are allowed. Do not be shy about including items that someone else might consider optional. Remember that the rooms must be sufficiently large to accommodate your furnishings. You will use this list to eliminate apartments that will not meet your basic needs.

✔ Define the geographic area that would be acceptable to you

The area you define must be a comfortable area for you to live and accessible to your regular destinations, particularly your work. Be sure that good and safe access is available during all possible hours of travel.

Do not gamble about commuting time—try it. And be sure to try it both ways during the rush hour. Do not listen to landlords and brokers about commuting times—they may lie. Be sure to also visit the area at night. Some neighborhoods tend to look very different after dark.

☑ Walk around the area you are considering and read signs and newspaper ads about apartments in it

You should have an idea about how many apartments are available and how much rent is charged for different apartments before you begin looking. There is no point in looking at apartments that will destroy your budget. They will only tempt you into something you cannot afford.

☑ Decide whether to use a real estate broker

A real estate broker who is familiar with a particular area and carries a good listing of apartments may be worthwhile. If you decide to use a broker, refer to the checklist for dealing with real estate brokers. Remember that using a broker who is tied to one or two landlords is the same as dealing with the landlords themselves. The point of a broker is to give you information and choices you could not easily obtain by talking to landlords.

☑ Check out everything in an apartment that interests you

Check the heat and hot water to be sure they are sufficient and reasonably quiet. Check to see that there is enough electricity for all your needs. If the apartment is in a building with a number of apartments, knock on one or two doors and ask the tenants how they find living in the building. Visit the building at different times of the day and night to see how you feel about it. If you have questions, ask the broker or landlord for answers. If you do not get answers or do not believe what you are told, look elsewhere.

Obtain a copy of the lease

Do not sign the lease until you have reviewed it thoroughly in accordance with the checklist for leases. (see pgs.86-87.) If there is something in the lease you do not understand, get someone to explain it to you. The lease is your contract to rent an apartment and you should not sign it until you are absolutely satisfied with it.

• • • • •

Dealing with Real Estate Brokers

A *real estate broker* familiar with the area in which you are interested, can save you a lot of time finding an apartment and usually can show you apartments that you would not find otherwise. Since landlords pay the commission of real estate brokers, using one should not cost you anything. If you are not able to get advice about a reliable real estate broker from a friend, relative, or co-worker, you will generally be able to identify real estate brokers who are active in a particular area from signs on rental properties. Choose a broker who makes sense and with whom you are comfortable. A good reference is always desirable if you can get one.

Checklist for Dealing with Real Estate Brokers

- ❏ Select a real estate broker familiar with apartment rentals in the area where you are interested
- ❏ Advise the real estate broker you select of your checklist for finding an apartment
- ❏ Do not enter a written contract with the real estate broker
- ❏ Do not rely on a real estate broker to check out an apartment for you
- ❏ Be sure the lease says that the broker's commission is to be paid by the landlord

✓ Select a real estate broker familiar with apartment rentals in the area where you are interested

Newspaper ads may be useful to determine which real estate brokers are active in particular areas. In general, real estate brokers who deal with apartment rentals are located in the areas where the apartments are located. If possible, choose a real estate broker who handles a number of buildings in a particular area for a number of landlords. While the bottom line for any real estate broker is his or her commission, brokers who represent a number of landlords will give you more unbiased information about the choices and comparisons.

✓ Advise the real estate broker you select of your checklist for finding an apartment

Since real estate brokers are paid by commission from the landlord, they do not particularly care what the tenant wants as long as they can rent an apartment. Make it clear to the real estate broker that your checklist is not negotiable and you do not want to look at any apartments that do not fit it.

If you feel the real estate broker is not showing you available apartments for any reason such as race, religion, nationality, or other personal characteristics, immediately report this to the appropriate state or federal authorities. This practice, known as *steering*, is thoroughly illegal.

☑ Do not enter a written contract with the real estate broker

Since the commission of a real estate broker is paid by the landlord, there is no reason for you to enter a contract with the broker. Most of the time the broker will not ask you to do so.

☑ Do not rely on a real estate broker to check out an apartment for you

Brokers care about landlords, since they may be repeat customers, while tenants are generally clients only once. All that brokers want to do is close the deal. Real estate brokers are not looking for reasons why you should not rent the apartment, so you have to check things out for yourself.

☑ Be sure that the lease says that the broker's commission is to be paid by the landlord

Real estate brokers who rent apartments are paid by landlords. (You will see this item on the checklist for your lease in the next section.)

• • • • •

Your Lease

The *lease* you sign for an apartment is a very important document. The lease establishes all of your rights as a tenant in the apartment and all of the rights of the landlord as well. Some apartment leases are relatively short forms that landlords purchase in various stores. Others are longer documents that have generally been prepared by lawyers. It does not matter to you whether your lease is a long or short document, provided it covers everything that is necessary for you.

The following checklist includes the items most tenants should be concerned about in their leases. A good part of most leases has to do with items like what the landlord can do if you do not pay your rent or what will happen if the building is destroyed or condemned. Since these items will almost surely not affect you and since they are almost never negotiable in any event, do not spend any time worrying about them.

Terms Used in Leases

- **assignment.** When a tenant transfers his rights to someone else.
- **common area.** The part of the building that is used by all tenants.
- **condominium.** A building in which each tenant owns his own apartment and shares the use of the common area.
- **cooperative (co-op).** A building in which each tenant owns stock in the corporation that owns the building and has a *proprietary lease* for his apartment.
- **demised premises.** The apartment that is leased to the tenant.
- **eviction.** The process of removing a tenant.
- **extension term (renewal term).** An additional period of time for which an apartment may be rented.
- **holding over.** Staying in a rented apartment after the lease has expired.
- **landlord.** The person or company who is renting the apartment to the tenant.

- **lease.** The contract between a landlord and a tenant.
- **real estate broker.** A person who leases apartments for landlords and receives an agreed commission for doing so.
- **renewal option.** A tenant's right to extend the term of a lease.
- **security deposit.** Money that a tenant pays and is held by the landlord in escrow in case the property is damaged.
- **sublease.** Lease between a tenant and someone who rents from the tenant.
- **tenant.** The person who is renting an apartment.
- **term.** The period of time for which an apartment is rented.

Checklist for Your Lease

❏ Be sure your lease accurately describes the place you are leasing
❏ Be sure your lease states precisely how long you are renting the apartment
❏ Be sure that the rent you will be paying is precisely what you understand
❏ Check your lease carefully to see what repairs you are responsible for making and what repairs are the landlord's responsibility
❏ Check to see what, if anything, you are required to do to the apartment and what you are prohibited from doing in it
❏ Be sure that if a real estate broker has been involved, your lease states that the landlord is solely responsible for the broker's fee

- ❏ See if the landlord will agree to place in your lease a provision entitling you to renew it
- ❏ Be sure that the provision in your lease regarding the *security deposit* is acceptable
- ❏ Obtain a fully executed copy of your lease

☑ Be sure your lease accurately describes the place you are leasing

The place you are leasing is called the *demised premises* in most leases. You must be sure that your lease describes precisely the place you are renting. If the apartment is in a multi-unit building, the floor and number of the apartment, or some other description that is absolutely clear, must be used. If any space outside the apartment is included, such as a storage facility or parking place, be sure that it is also mentioned in the lease. Oral promises are not enforceable once you have a written lease, so anything you are *told* may not be how it *is*. Your lease must fully describe everything you are getting.

☑ Be sure your lease states precisely how long you are renting the apartment

The length of time that you are renting is known in most leases as the *term*. Terms in leases are generally one or more years, but that is not always the case. Since both you and the landlord are committed for the term of the lease, you must be sure that you are willing to stay in the apartment for the whole time.

Be sure that the rent you will be paying is precisely what you understand

Some leases contain extra charges for things like taxes, insurance, or maintenance. You must check the whole lease to be sure that there are no extra charges you are not planning on paying. Leases of more than one year sometimes provide for slightly higher rent in subsequent years. As a general rule, an increase of up to five percent per year is in the ballpark. Prepare yourself for increases in rent. If you will be parking your car on your landlord's property, be sure you know whether there is an extra charge for parking.

 Check your lease carefully to see what repairs you are responsible for making and what repairs are the landlord's responsibility

You should be responsible for very little if anything in this regard, unless you break something. In no event should you be responsible for anything outside the apartment, such as the building's central heat, air conditioning, or common utilities (such as hallway or outside lighting). Be careful also that your lease does not make you responsible for things like leaks that may come through the apartment from the outside.

 Check to see what, if anything, you are required to do to the apartment and what you are prohibited from doing in it

Some leases require tenants to do certain things. For example, some leases require the tenant to cover a certain percentage of the floor area with rugs or carpeting. You should check your lease carefully to determine what you are required to do in the apartment.

Many leases also prohibit tenants from doing certain things. If you have a pet, this is something to be checked carefully. Check to see whether your lease prohibits hanging pictures, painting walls, or doing other things that you will want to do in your apartment.

 Be sure that if a real estate broker has been involved, your lease states that the landlord is solely responsible for the broker's fee

If no broker has been involved insofar as you are concerned, your lease should state that no broker was utilized, and if any broker claims the right to a commission, the party who engaged the broker will pay it. The reason for this is that landlords sometimes have arrangements with brokers that are unknown to tenants.

 See if the landlord will agree to place in your lease a provision entitling you to renew it

A *renewal option*, which must establish the rent during the renewal term, is a very useful item for any tenant. For example, if you have a one-year lease and have the right to renew it for another year, you are only committed for the one-year period, but are protected from being evicted or having to pay a much higher rent in the second year if you decide to stay. If you can get a renewal option, take it and be certain that you understand the notice requirements for exercising it. Calendar the notice date carefully, since you will forego your option if you miss it.

 Be sure that the provision in your lease regarding the security deposit is acceptable

Generally, security deposits are equal to one month's rent. If the security deposit is larger than that, you should ask the landlord to reduce it. Although state laws are strict about how landlords must treat security deposits, your lease should state that the security deposit will be returned to you, minus any expense for repairs or unpaid rent, within a very short time after you vacate the apartment.

☑ Obtain a fully executed copy of your lease
It is important that you receive a copy of your lease fully completed and signed by both parties. If anything on the typewritten lease is changed in handwriting, both parties should initial the change to show that it has been agreed to. Keep your copy of the lease in a safe place, since you may need it at a later time.

• • • • •

Complaints and Requests
Hopefully, you will not need to have many interactions with your landlord or the manager of your building after you move in. Unfortunately, this is not always the case. Tenants have to deal with their landlords because of problems in their apartments or the building generally. When this occurs, it is important to follow the correct procedure so that the difficulty can be resolved as quickly and easily as possible. Identify the person responsible for the care of the building as soon as you move into your apartment. If you have a complaint or request thereafter, use the following checklist as your guide to handle it.

Checklist for Complaints and Requests

❏ Make a telephone call to the person responsible for taking care of the building, requesting whatever is needed, and record the date and time of the phone call
❏ Send the landlord or the landlord's agent a typewritten letter making your request absolutely clear
❏ File a case in landlord-tenant court, following the directions of the court's clerk

☑ Make a telephone call to the person responsible for taking care of the building, requesting whatever is needed, and record the date and time of the phone call

In small buildings, the person responsible for taking care of the building may be the landlord and not some other building manager. Every building has some person in charge of answering complaints and making repairs. As you would expect, landlords have a much greater interest in receiving checks than in responding to complaints and requests for repairs. Make yourself absolutely clear with regard to what you are requesting. Keep a record of the request so that you can use it in any necessary later communication. If the matter is urgent, such as a loss of heat or hot or cold water, tell the person that you need to have the repair made immediately, since you cannot live in the apartment without it.

☑ Send the landlord or the landlord's agent a typewritten letter making your request absolutely clear

This letter should be sent by certified mail, return receipt requested, so that the landlord will know you are serious and you will have proof of the letter being delivered. Refer in your letter to the telephone call previously made. Do not include any extras in the letter, but make it clear that you expect a prompt response. You can make a threat to go to landlord-tenant court in your letter, but you might want to save this for a follow-up letter if the first one does not work.

A sample complaint letter is provided for your reference.

Sample Complaint Letter to Landlord

23 Woodbridge Lane, Apt. 403
Albany, New York 00000

May 27, 2005

CERTIFIED MAIL
RETURN RECEIPT REQUESTED

Mr. Seymour L. Carter
Woodbridge Management Co.
26 Royal Street
Albany, New York 00000

Re: 23 Woodbridge Lane, Apt. 403
Albany, New York 00000

Dear Mr. Carter:

As you know, I am the tenant in Apartment 403 at Woodbridge Gardens. I have lived here for 14 months and have a three-year lease.

Over a week ago, on May 17, 2005, I telephoned your office to advise your manager that the refrigerator in my apartment was not maintaining a constant temperature. Nothing was done in response to my call and I telephoned your office again three days later, on May 20, 2005. Once again, nothing was done. I am writing to demand that my refrigerator be repaired promptly or replaced with a new refrigerator. The food in my apartment has spoiled on several occasions and I am losing money as a result.

My lease entitles me to have the appliances that were supplied with my apartment in working order. The refrigerator is one of those appliances. If it is not repaired or replaced within the next week, I will be forced to spend my own money to remedy the problem. If I have to do so, I will deduct the amount I must spend from my next month's rent.

I am sorry to have to write this letter, but this matter is interfering with the use of my apartment.

Sincerely,
Jane M. Withers

☑ **File a case in landlord-tenant court, following the directions of the court's clerk**

Landlord-tenant court is a last resort if letters and telephone calls do not work. The clerk of the court will help you complete the appropriate documents. If you have written a letter requesting the repairs, attach a copy to the court papers so that the judge will have it when your case comes up. If a photograph would be a good way to show a problem, take one and ask the clerk how to present it to the court. In most instances, you do not need a lawyer in landlord-tenant court. The judges expedite the cases as much as possible. Frequently, filing the complaint and having it served on the landlord will accomplish your purpose without the need for you to go through a court hearing.

• • • • •

Dealing with a Roommate

A roommate can be your best friend or worst enemy. Sometimes a roommate starts out as one and becomes the other. To make sure that your situation does not turn sour, take these precautions.

Checklist for Dealing with a Roommate

- ❏ Resolve all issues about living in the same apartment with your roommate before you sign your lease
- ❏ Have your roommate sign the lease, if you want him or her to be responsible for rent
- ❏ Work out a system with your roommate for getting the rent together a few days before it is due

Resolve all issues about living in the same apartment with your roommate before you sign your lease

Be sure you agree with your roommate about things like smoking, alcohol and drugs, guests, hours for sleeping, music, and everything else that may affect your lifestyle. Nothing in the law will help you if you get a roommate whose personal habits do not work for you. Be sure, also, that your roommate is financially responsible, since you do not want to be running after him or her for rent.

 Have your roomate signs the lease, if you want him or her to be responsible for rent

A private deal between you and a roommate is not binding on your landlord. In general, tenants who sign a lease together are *jointly and severally* responsible for the rent. This means that the landlord may go after either tenant for the entire rent and it is the tenants' problem to divide responsibility between themselves.

 Work out a system with your roommate for getting the rent together a few days before it is due

Some roommates are always unavailable when rent becomes due. This is an aggravation you can live without. Get this matter straight in the beginning and stick to the script.

• • • • •

Apartment Insurance

As a tenant in an apartment, you will need to obtain apartment insurance. You should do this as soon as you sign your lease, so that you will have the insurance when you move into your apartment.

Apartment insurance protects you against the destruction or theft of your personal property in the apartment, and it also protects you if someone is injured in the apartment.

> ## Terms Used in Apartment Insurance Policies
>
> - **deductible.** The amount of a loss you must pay before insurance coverage takes over.
> - **floater coverage.** Coverage for your property when you take it out of the apartment.
> - **limits of liability.** The maximum amount the insurance company will pay for damages.
> - **personal injury liability.** Coverage for injury to other persons while visiting your apartment.
> - **personal property rider.** Insurance coverage for specific items such as silverware or artworks that are very valuable.
> - **property damage.** Damage to your possessions due to fire, theft or malicious mischief.
> - **renter's insurance. (apartment insurance).** Liability and property insurance for an apartment.

Checklist for Apartment Insurance

- ❏ Select a good, independent insurance broker
- ❏ Choose an insurance company that has a high rating
- ❏ Select an insurance policy with sufficient liability coverage and sufficient property damage or loss coverage
- ❏ Obtain an insurance policy with deductibles not larger than what you can comfortably afford
- ❏ Obtain a copy of your apartment insurance policy

✓ Select a good, independent insurance broker

An independent insurance broker is one who does not work for, or limit association to, one particular company. An independent insurance broker can give you a few choices and a few different insurance costs from different companies.

✓ Choose an insurance company that has a high rating

Insurance companies are rated by several rating companies, particularly *A.M. Best's*, *Moody's*, and *Standard and Poor*. You want a company with a high rating. Your insurance broker will be able to advise you on the rating of the companies he or she gives you quotes from.

✓ Select an insurance policy with sufficient liability coverage and sufficient property damage or loss coverage

Apartment insurance, which is sometimes called *renter's insurance*, serves two purposes. It protects you against liabilities that could arise if someone is injured in your apartment and it protects the property in your apartment against losses due to damage or theft. Apartment insurance does not provide coverage for a rental apartment itself, since you do not own it. Instead, it covers the things you own in it and protects you if someone is hurt in your apartment.

The liability part of your policy should be at least $100,000 and the property damage or loss part of your policy should be sufficient to cover the value of all of your property. Good apartment insurance has a provision that covers property damage or loss outside of the apartment up to a particular amount. This coverage might apply to theft of or damage to property you take on a trip or carry in your car. If this is important to you, read this provision carefully and, if necessary, discuss it with your broker.

✓ Obtain an insurance policy with deductibles not larger than you can comfortably afford

Deductibles are the amount of a claim you must pay yourself before the insurance takes over. You apartment insurance policy will have deductibles for both liability and property damage or loss. The higher the deductibles, the lower the cost of the policy. However, the higher the deductible, the more you must pay out-of-pocket before the insurance will kick in.

✓ Obtain a copy of your apartment insurance policy

Always obtain a copy of any insurance policy you purchase. Do not settle for a summary, but insist upon a copy of the policy itself.

• • • • •

Making a Claim under Your Apartment Insurance Policy

If you suffer a loss that is covered by your apartment insurance policy, you should be certain to do exactly what is necessary to make a valid claim. Insurance companies are not looking for ways to pay money to policy holders, but they will honor valid claims nearly all the time if they are presented correctly. Take the steps in the following checklist if you need to make a claim.

Checklist for Making a Claim under Your Apartment Insurance Policy

- ❑ Read the procedure for making a claim set forth in your apartment insurance policy
- ❑ Notify the police immediately
- ❑ Obtain a copy of the police report
- ❑ Verify the value of all items that were stolen, damaged, or destroyed
- ❑ Advise the insurance company of the specific amount of your claim
- ❑ Write a certified mail, return receipt requested, letter to the insurance company, stating exactly your position if it will not pay a satisfactory amount
- ❑ Check with your state's insurance commission to see if it can be of assistance if you cannot come to an agreement with your insurance company

☑ Read the procedure for making a claim set forth in your apartment insurance policy

You must follow the instructions for making a claim precisely. It is permissible to ask your insurance broker to notify the insurance company. Ask your insurance broker to explain any procedures you do not understand or have questions about. As with all insurance matters, do not discuss anything with anyone other than your own broker and your own insurance company.

Notify the police immediately

Failure to notify the police may destroy an insurance claim. Provide full and complete information to the police so that the police report will be thoroughly accurate.

 Obtain a copy of the police report

In most instances, police reports are available within a few days. You can obtain a copy from the police officer that took the report.

To save time, provide a copy of the police report to your insurance broker or the insurance company itself.

 Verify the value of all items that were stolen, damaged, or destroyed

Bills of sale and appraisals are particularly useful for this purpose. Of course, insurance companies are aware that used items are worth less than new ones. You may need to utilize an appraiser or someone else with experience to establish the value of certain items. Unfortunately, insurance companies tend to go by the used value of an item and not the cost of replacing it with a new item. It is possible to obtain insurance that will pay the *replacement cost* of certain items, but it is more expensive.

 Advise the insurance company of the specific amount of your claim

A phone call will do for this purpose in most instances. If an insurance appraiser visits you, you should be prepared to advise the appraiser of the value of your claim and provide the appropriate documents.

Write a certified mail, return receipt requested, letter to the insurance company, stating exactly your position if it will not pay a satisfactory amount

A letter of this type should be fully documented with receipts and any other materials showing the value of property that was lost. If you do not have any such items, some form of valuation, such as a sales notice regarding comparable items, may be helpful.

A sample letter is provided.

Sample Letter to Apartment Insurance Company

Apt. No. 6
Garden Terrace Apartments
Nashville, Tennessee 00000

February 14, 2005

CERTIFIED MAIL
RETURN RECEIPT REQUESTED

Ms. Holly Simpkins
Landmark Insurance Company
1273 Newtown Road
Belair, Tennessee 00000

Re: Apt. No. 6
Garden Terrace Apartments
Nashville, Tennessee 00000
Policy No. 27963BD

Dear Ms. Simpkins:

As you know, I am the tenant of Apt. No. 6 at Garden Terrace Apartments and have an insurance policy with your company. On January 14, 2005, my apartment was robbed. You have been furnished with a copy of the police report. The items stolen are as follows: 30" Sony color television; Sony VCR; Yamaha receiver and CD player; 2 wrist watches; and a pair of gold earrings. As the enclosed receipts verify, these items were purchased very recently at a total value of $2,873.67.

Your offer to settle this matter for $1,250.00 is absolutely unacceptable. I will settle the matter for $2,000.00 if we can do so promptly. If not, I will pursue my legal remedies.

Sincerely,
Sandra Buchanan

Enclosures

Check with your state's insurance commission to see if it can be of assistance if you cannot come to an agreement with your insurance company

Most states have agencies set up to provide assistance in insurance claims. The appropriate office for this purpose is listed in your telephone book in the government pages. If you have a substantial dispute with an insurance company, you may wish to seek legal assistance.

CHAPTER 5

Automobiles

When it comes to buying and owning a car, a lot more goes into it than you might think. In fact, one of the first things you should do if contemplating getting a car is to ask yourself, *Should I buy a car?*

If, after examining the costs of owning a car, you still want to buy one, this chapter will take you through several checklists regarding buying a car, financing your purchase, getting it insured, and what to do in case of an accident.

Should I Buy A Car?

The first thing you must determine regarding a car is whether to buy one. Part of this decision depends upon the cost of owning a car and part of it depends upon how you lead your life and how much you would like to own a car. If you live in a crowded city, you would not be the first person to learn the hard way that your life may be easier without a car. If you live in a small or middle-size community with no public transportation, you might not have any choice about the matter. Whatever you decide, do not fool yourself about the cost involved. The following checklist will help you determine the realistic cost of owning a car.

Checklist of Costs of Owning a Car

- ❏ Purchase price
- ❏ Monthly expenses
    - ❏ Insurance
    - ❏ Gas and oil
    - ❏ Repairs and general maintenance
    - ❏ Parking and garage expenses
    - ❏ Tolls
    - ❏ State inspections
    - ❏ Registration fees
    - ❏ Car washes

✓ Purchase price

The first consideration for anybody who is thinking about owning a car is money. Most people can be reasonably certain about the cost of transportation without a car. People commute to and from work on the same predictable routes. People tend to average out their transportation costs to see friends and doctors and go to special places they visit fairly often. But it is more difficult to determine how much buying and using a car will cost you. If you think of this in terms of a monthly payment plus a few bucks here and there for gas, you are kidding yourself and you will quickly find out why.

    A good thing to know if you are planning on buying a new car is how much the car you want to buy costs the dealer. This is not as easy to determine as you might think. The *sticker price* of the car is worthless in this regard. All stickers show prices that are inflated and, in some cases, very inflated. There are books available in many bookstores called *Pace Buyer's Guides* that give dealer prices for all kinds of new cars. In addition, there are websites that provide dealer cost information on automobiles. Three of these are **www.edmunds.com**, **www.autoquote.com**, and **www.carprice.com**.

Dealers make a profit on new cars not only by selling them for more than the price of the invoice the car manufacturer gives the dealer, but also by an agreed *holdback*, which is an amount of money the dealer does not have to pay to the manufacturer even though it is included in the invoice price. To make matters more complicated, dealers often have more than one invoice showing what they refer to as the *true book price* of a new car. By looking at the *Pace* books or one of the websites, you will be able to tell which of the invoices a dealer shows you is the correct invoice.

The cost of buying a car includes the price of the car, the price of inspecting it if you purchase a used car, the sales tax, the titling and registration fees, and sometimes other costs, such as an extended warranty. If you finance your car, this cost will break down into a *down payment* and a *monthly payment* for a certain number of years.

Another way to look at it is in terms of the amount of money you will lose if you own the car for a certain period of time. If you buy a new car, you will lose more money the first year than in any other year. New cars go down in price a good deal for the first year or two. One way to look at the cost of buying a car is to determine how much its value will go down over a period of years. Many people use five years as the period for this purpose, even though they may own their cars for longer periods of time.

You can get a good idea of the decrease in value of your car over a five-year period by comparing its price at the time you buy it to the price of similar cars five years older. One way to obtain such prices is to look at the *Blue Book*, which most car dealers have available and will show you. Another way is to check ads in your local newspaper. If your local newspaper is not a major city newspaper, try to get one as there are many more car listings in big newspapers.

☑ Monthly expenses

Once you have determined the monthly cost of buying your car, whether you use the monthly payment or the monthly depreciation method, you must also determine the monthly cost of using it. Divide the annual cost of your car insurance by twelve and you have the monthly cost of car insurance. For gas and oil, check with someone whose driving habits are pretty much like yours and ask how much he or she spends on these things each month. Depending on the age and style of your car, you will also have to allow a monthly amount for repairs. This is something that also can be determined from someone who drives a similar car.

Do not forget to include periodic registration fees for new license plates, or new stickers for your existing license plates, as well as periodic state-required inspection fees. If you have to pay a monthly parking fee for your car, either where you live or where you work, be sure to include the monthly fee. Now add a few extra dollars for car washes, tolls, and a few other things you will buy in connection with your car from time to time. Add up all of these costs on a monthly basis and you have the approximate cost per month of using your car. Add the monthly cost of using your car to the monthly cost of buying it and you have the monthly cost of car ownership.

NOTE: *Remember that you are entitled to deduct from your taxable income the business expense of utilizing a car when it is not reimbursed by your employer. As of January 1, 2004, the IRS set a rate of 37.5¢ per mile for the business use of a private car.*

• • • • •

Buying a Car

If you have decided to own a car and have realistically considered the costs involved, you are ready to begin the process of buying your car. You will be dealing with people who go through this process every day, but you should not be intimidated by them. If someone rushes you or does not want to answer all your questions, find someone else to deal with. You can be sure that there is no shortage of people available for every step in the process of buying a car. Use the following checklist for the items you need to address to make this important purchase.

Checklist for Buying a Car

- ❏ Determine the type of car you want to buy
- ❏ Arrange financing if you require it
- ❏ Get the car inspected by an independent mechanic before you sign the contract
- ❏ Verify that the necessary state inspections are up-to-date
- ❏ Verify that car insurance is affordable
- ❏ Purchase automobile insurance
- ❏ Arrange for parking and garaging at necessary locations
- ❏ Verify that the car is properly registered at the time of its purchase

✓ Determine the type of car you want to buy

Selecting a car is a little like selecting a friend or mate. You need to decide the make, model, size, color, cost, cost of repairs, and age of the car that is suitable for you. If you have a bad back, the seating of a car may be a major item to you. If you have a wife and two children and drive with them all the time, four doors instead of two may be a big ticket item. For some people, the color of a car makes a great deal of difference. Other people could care less about a car's color (unless it is shocking pink).

Decide what things you absolutely have to have in a car before you go shopping. Also decide the general price range you can afford. If you want to spend about $10,000 on a reasonably new small car with basic features, you can skip the dealers that sell $45,000 cars with satellite-tracking systems and leather seats with built-in trays.

NOTE: *Remember when considering whether to buy a new or used car that cars depreciate very quickly in the first year or two.*

Arrange financing if you require it
The subject of financing is discussed on page 110.

Get the car inspected by an independent mechanic before you sign the contract
This subject is discussed on pages 111-113.

Verify that the necessary state inspections are up-to-date
Various states require various forms of automobile inspection on a periodic basis. These include safety, emission control, and other forms of inspections. You can obtain these requirements easily by calling your state's department of motor vehicles. Generally, stickers on windshields or license plates indicate the most recent inspections. Be certain that all required state inspections of a car you intend to buy are up-to-date.

Verify that car insurance is affordable
Proper car insurance is essential for owning an automobile. Bear in mind when shopping for a new car that certain types of cars, for example sports cars and SUVs, often have higher insurance costs associated with them.

Purchase automobile insurance

The subject of auto insurance is discussed more fully on pages 113-118.

 Arrange for parking and garaging at necessary locations

You would not be the first person to learn that suitable parking, either near your home or place of work, is not available. Parking places in congested areas are very often fully utilized and there are substantial waiting periods for them in some instances. Since you will surely want to keep your car near your home and use it for commuting to work at least some of the time, this is an important matter to verify before purchasing a car.

 Verify that the car is properly registered at the time of its purchase

Automobiles must be registered in order to be driven. In some states, *title* to automobiles, which means ownership, takes place through the registration process. In other states, there are separate titles and registrations for automobiles. Whatever may be the case in your state, you must be sure that everything necessary is accomplished for your car. Automobile dealers, new and used, customarily take care of all this paperwork for new buyers. If you are not buying your car from a dealer, however, you should check with your state department of motor vehicles and be certain to obtain all documentation it requires in order for your car to be registered and titled to you.

• • • • •

Financing the Purchase of a Car

Of all the things you can buy, a car is probably the easiest to buy with borrowed money. Nearly every car dealer, new and used, has connections with one or more banks or finance companies that loan money to buy cars. Most banks and finance companies will also loan money to you if you buy a car from a private individual, provided you complete the required paperwork.

Although the amount of money you must put down (the *down payment*) varies with different cars, different dealers, and different lenders—cars are generally an easy purchase to finance. Even people who have little credit or less-than-perfect credit may be able to finance a car. There are two main reasons for this. One is that there are more banks and other lenders available for cars than any other type of purchase. More competition means that loans that might not otherwise be made will be. The other is that cars are good security for lenders.

When you finance a car, what is known as a *lien* is placed on it by the lender. To do so, the lender records in the appropriate state offices—one of which is the Department of Motor Vehicles—the fact that it has a claim on your car. You cannot legally sell your car unless the lien is removed or paid. In addition to this, cars are relatively easy for lenders to *repossess* or take away from you to pay off your loan. A car is a hard thing to hide, especially when its location and license plate number are known.

When you compare possible loans for your car, there are several things to look for. You should look at the required down payment, since you will have to pay that amount to get the loan. Also look at the interest rate that applies to the loan, the monthly payment you are required to make, and the number of months (the *term*) for which you are required to make payments.

Lenders are required to advise you of the interest rate in what is known as the *annual percentage rate* (APR). This is the rate of interest that a loan requires you to pay each year. The lower the APR, the less interest you will pay. Once you know how much of your car's purchase price you will be financing, you can compare loans by comparing the interest rates, the monthly payments, and the terms. If the loans you are comparing are for the same amount of money, you will be able to tell which loan is better from these comparisons.

Loan documents tend to be a little complicated, but their purpose is quite simple. You are borrowing a certain amount of money to purchase a car and you agree to repay the money plus interest in certain monthly payments for a stated number of months. You agree to make a certain down payment. You are giving the lender two things to assure it that it will be repaid. One is your personal obligation to repay it and the other is a lien on the car. The lender will require you to keep the car fully insured since it is the security for the loan.

• • • • •

Car Inspections

Most states require one or more forms of regular inspection of cars. Even if you live in a state that is very strict in this regard, you should definitely have the car you propose to buy inspected for you by someone who is qualified to do so. Recent inspection stickers from state-approved facilities and Internet services that provide information about the history of cars are not an adequate substitute for an inspection by your own mechanic before you sign a contract to buy a car.

Checklist for Car Inspections

- ❑ Do not have your car inspected by anyone associated with the person trying to sell it to you
- ❑ Use a mechanic who is familiar with the kind of car you are buying
- ❑ Be sure the inspection provision in your contract of sale is sufficient

Do not have your car inspected by anyone associated with the person trying to sell it to you

There is no sense in having a car (or anything else) inspected by anyone associated with the person trying to sell it to you. If you are buying a car from a used car dealer that is associated with a new car dealer, do not use the new car dealer's mechanic to inspect the car for you. Their loyalty will be to the dealership, which wants to make a sale, and not to you.

 Use a mechanic who is familiar with the kind of car you are buying

It is essential that you use a mechanic who is familiar with the kind of car you are buying and will spend sufficient time to look it over carefully. If the car needs to be taken a reasonable distance to get it inspected properly, make arrangements with the seller for that to be done. If the seller will not cooperate with you, go to a different dealer.

 Be sure the inspection provision in your contract of sale is sufficient

Many people and most dealers want to have a sales contract before they spend time arranging for a car to be inspected. This is satisfactory, provided you are prepared to buy the car if the inspection goes well and provided the contract contains a provision that clearly says that *the sale is conditioned upon a satisfactory inspection in the buyer's discretion*. It is very important that the contract provision not simply say that the inspection must be satisfactory, because this is a matter that could be disputed. The contract provision must say that the inspection must be satisfactory in your discretion. It should also say that if the inspection is not satisfactory in your discretion, any deposit you have paid will be returned and the contract ended. You do not need to get into legalese to be sure that your contract contains this kind of provision. If it is there, you should be able to identify it and read it correctly. If it is not there, do not let a car dealer or anyone else convince you that you are getting these rights.

• • • • •

Automobile Insurance

Whatever the requirements of your state may be, the question of whether to get automobile insurance is indisputable. Owning (or even driving) a car without appropriate automobile insurance is probably the best way to risk ending your financial life. The cost of even the most minor injuries to other people can be very large. The cost of inflicting serious injuries on a person is often gigantic. Medical bills alone, not to mention damages for pain and suffering and lost income, could bankrupt even a wealthy person. Even an accident in which no one is hurt can be a big expense if you hit an expensive car or someone's property.

You may think that you will never have an accident because you drive with extraordinary care. Even if you are the world's safest driver and never make a mistake while you are driving, you may have to contend with claims from other drivers.

Example: One day you enter an intersection on a green light and to your shock see a car coming at you from your right, obviously going through the red light. The car collides with you damaging both cars and injuring you and the other driver. When you get out of the hospital two days later there is a surprising visitor waiting for you at your apartment. The visitor is a deputy sheriff and he has come to serve a complaint on you that was filed by the other driver. The complaint says that you were negligent, ran a red light, and collided with the other driver's car. It says that you have caused the other driver to suffer a back injury, which his doctor says will give him a permanent disability. The complaint asks that you be required by the court to pay damages for the injuries to the other driver, including medical bills, physical therapy, loss of income, pain and suffering, loss of his car, and a few other things his clever lawyer has thrown in for the heck of it. What do you do now?

If you have automobile insurance, the answer to this question is simple. You telephone your insurance company or its representative and send them the complaint you have received immediately. Your insurance company is required to provide you with a competent lawyer to defend the claims being made against you. (You will certainly not have any trouble finding a lawyer to make your own claims against the other driver.) But if you do not have automobile insurance, you would be in for a very rude shock. You would have to hire and pay a lawyer to defend you even though you know full well that you did absolutely nothing wrong. One of the most important reasons why every driver needs to be covered by adequate automobile insurance is that automobile insurance pays not only for claims against you if they are successful but also for a lawyer to defend you, whether the claims are successful or not.

Just as with every form of insurance, you should be certain to obtain automobile insurance from a well-rated insurance company. You can get rates for automobile insurance from each company, agent, or broker that sells it. You should use an independent broker that sells different types of automobile insurance to give you rates of different companies and perhaps a good recommendation about the best company for you. The insurance coverage provided by automobile insurance policies has a number of components.

Checklist of Components of Automobile Insurance

- ❏ Bodily injury liability
- ❏ Property damage liability
- ❏ Comprehensive coverage
- ❏ Collision coverage
- ❏ Uninsured motorists coverage
- ❏ Personal injury protection
- ❏ Emergency road service coverage
- ❏ Temporary car rental coverage

☑ Bodily injury liability

This is the most important item of comparison for automobile insurance policies. *Bodily injury liability* is the amount the insurance company will pay for injuries to other people caused by negligent driving. In most instances, automobile insurance policies have two bodily injury liability limits. One is known as the *per-person* limit and the other is known as the *per-occurrence* limit.

The per-person limit is the maximum amount the insurance company will pay to each injured person in an accident. The per-occurrence limit is the maximum amount the insurance company will pay for an entire accident. Sometimes the per-person and per-occurrence liability limits of an automobile insurance policy are the same and sometimes they are different. In most instances in which they are different, the per-occurrence liability limit is twice the per-person limit.

If someone says that they have a *50/100* automobile insurance policy, they are saying that the per-person liability limit of their policy is $50,000 and the per-occurrence liability limit is $100,000. Since higher bodily injury liability limits are generally not much more expensive than lower ones, it is advisable to get the highest possible bodily injury liability limits. Sometimes, because of age, driving record, or other factors, only minimum bodily injury liability limits are available to you. If this is the case, you have no choice but to accept those limits or not own a car.

 Property damage liability

Each automobile insurance policy also has a *property damage liability* limit. This applies to injuries to someone else's automobile or other property. The property damage liability limit is always much lower than the bodily injury liability limit. Since most accidents involving damage to property involve damage to another vehicle, there is not as much risk involved with regard to property damage as there is with regard to bodily injury.

 Comprehensive coverage

Comprehensive coverage in an automobile insurance policy protects your vehicle and sometimes property that is in it from theft or other forms of damage.

 Collision coverage

Collision coverage protects your automobile in the event it is damaged in an accident. Both comprehensive coverage and collision coverage are subject to what is known as a *deductible*. A deductible is the amount of the loss that is not paid for by the insurance policy. As a general rule, the higher the deductible, the lower the cost or *premium* for the insurance. If you have a car that is worth little or nothing, these forms of insurance are not worth paying for. If you do get either or both of them, get reasonably high deductibles because you can probably take a certain amount of risk yourself in return for a lower premium. Follow the rule that you buy insurance for risks you cannot afford to take.

Uninsured motorists coverage

Many automobile insurance policies provide coverage for what is known as *uninsured motorists*. In many states, it is required that automobile insurance policies provide this coverage. This coverage protects you and your passengers from personal injuries due to another motorist who does not have insurance or has insufficient insurance.

Uninsured motorists coverage also provides property damage coverage to you for your car if it is damaged by such a motorist. Uninsured motorists coverage is generally not expensive and you should get it whether or not your state requires it. You can usually get uninsured motorists coverage for bodily injuries and property damage with the same liability limits as apply to your automobile insurance policy in general.

 Personal injury protection

Personal injury protection (PIP) insurance provides medical expense coverage to you and sometimes your passengers regardless of who caused an accident. Some states also require this form of protection. Like uninsured motorists coverage, PIP coverage is relatively inexpensive. Get it even if your state does not require it.

 Emergency road service coverage

Emergency road service coverage is that which pays for road service or towing up to certain amounts. This coverage is not terribly important, but it is usually very inexpensive. The decision is yours as to whether or not you buy this coverage.

 Temporary car rental coverage

This insurance provides you with money to rent a car for a limited period of time if your car is damaged in an accident. If an accident is caused by someone else, you will generally receive money for this purpose from the other person's insurance company. This coverage is useful, however, when the accident is your fault or where fault is disputed. It is generally inexpensive.

The premiums for automobile insurance are usually paid more than once a year. Some policies provide for payment every six months, some for payment every three months and a few for payment every month. The important thing for you is your total annual automobile insurance premium and your monthly automobile insurance premium, which is $\frac{1}{12}$ of it. Since this will be a big expense for you, be sure to get straight the payment terms of whatever automobile insurance policy you buy.

• • • • •

Accidents

The way you handle an accident may affect your finances, your future driving record, and your relations with automobile insurance companies. If you have an accident and handle it correctly, the chances of adverse consequences to you are reduced considerably. The key to handling an accident properly is good insurance coverage and knowledge of the steps to take if you have an accident. Be sure to carry an insurance card with your registration card in the car so that you will have the insurance company's contact information and directions about whom you should contact in the case of an accident.

Checklist for Handling Accidents

- ☐ Get good medical care for anyone injured
- ☐ Cooperate with police, but do not make unnecessary admissions
- ☐ Provide the other driver with identifying and insurance information
- ☐ Obtain identifying and insurance information from the other driver
- ☐ Obtain identification from any witnesses to the accident
- ☐ Advise your insurance company promptly and cooperate with it
- ☐ Do not provide information to lawyers or insurance representatives for other parties
- ☐ Obtain a copy of the police report

☑ Get good medical care for anyone injured

Before attending to any of the business matters of an accident, be certain that medical care is acquired for anyone who is injured. If you have a cellular telephone, use it and call 911 immediately. If not, ask someone in the vicinity or even the other driver to assist you. The person who does not do everything possible to get medical care immediately for someone who needs it has a very hard time explaining that in any legal proceedings that may follow.

☑ Cooperate with police, but do not make unnecessary admissions

If a police officer comes to the scene of the accident, either because you or someone else telephoned for one, or an officer arrives for some other reason, you must provide full information to the officer to the extent it is requested. Do not, however, make admissions about the accident since these will almost always appear in the police report that is available to either side after a very short while. The police officer may make a determination about who caused the accident, but there is nothing you can do about that. If the other driver says things that are favorable to you, the police officer may put them in the police report and you should, in any event, make notes about them. Do not do this until after the other driver has left, however, since you do not want him or her to change his or her story.

 Provide the other driver with identifying and insurance information

Provide the other driver with your name, address, telephone number, insurance company, policy number, and insurance company's telephone number.

NOTE: *Do not make any admissions regarding the accident to the other driver, even if you feel you were at fault.*

 Obtain identifying and insurance information from the other driver

You should receive from the other driver precisely the same information that you provide to him or her. If you have any question about the information being provided to you, ask to see the other driver's license. Regardless of what information you are given by the other driver, be sure to write down the other driver's license plate number and a general description of his or her car. If there are other people in the other driver's car, be sure to write down each person's name, address, and telephone number.

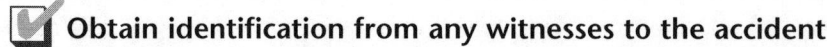 **Obtain identification from any witnesses to the accident**

If there are people nearby who were witnesses to the accident, ask them if they will provide their names and telephone numbers to you. If it is reasonably certain that the accident is the other person's fault, this information will be particularly valuable.

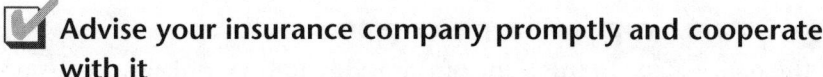 **Advise your insurance company promptly and cooperate with it**

The only people you should speak with following an accident are representatives of your own insurance company and the lawyer who is selected by your insurance company to represent you. Be sure to verify his or her identity before you say anything to one of those persons. The other side may be trying to get you to disclose something that will later hurt your case. Your insurance policy requires you to cooperate fully with your own insurance company and its lawyer, but not anyone else. This requirement is set forth in what is known as the *cooperation clause* of your insurance policy.

If a lawsuit is filed and not settled immediately, you will probably be involved in different forms of paperwork and a deposition before it is over. Your lawyer will instruct you about each of these matters and there is nothing for you to worry about. Prompt advice to your insurance company is required by your insurance policy in order for your coverage to be effective.

Do not provide information to lawyers or insurance representatives for the other parties

It is very common after an accident for someone representing the other person involved to telephone you. The caller may be a lawyer representing the other person or someone working for the other person's insurance company. Regardless of who the caller is, do not provide any information whatsoever to that person. Bear in mind that even your best efforts to explain the matter in your favor may be used against you in some clever way. The correct and only statement to make to such a person is:

> *I cannot discuss the accident with you at all. Please do not call me again. Goodbye.*

☑ Obtain a copy of the police report

If the police come to the scene of the accident, they will almost always prepare a police report. This report will be available at the station house or precinct from which the police officers came, generally in a few days to a week after the accident. In many instances, your insurance company will obtain a copy of the report, but it does no harm for you to obtain it as well.

If you feel that the accident was the other party's fault and you have injuries or other damages to you or your car and its contents, you will need to obtain legal assistance for your claim. Your insurance company's obligation is to defend you, not to bring claims on your behalf, even if you are clearly entitled to make them.

If you feel you have a claim for injuries or damages, find yourself a good lawyer who represents people in car accidents on a regular basis. Some of these lawyers advertise themselves in various places, but they are not necessarily the best. Check with your friends and any people you know who may have used such a lawyer. Once you have chosen a lawyer, be sure to advise him or her of the insurance company's role in regard to the accident and the lawyer the insurance company has chosen to represent you if that has occurred. It is unfortunate that you may need two lawyers, one to defend you and the other to make your claims, as a result of a single accident. But if you follow the instructions of each lawyer and your case is good, you should wind up with a satisfactory result.

There is one other thing to be aware of with regard to accidents. If you or the other party is given a ticket as a result of the accident, the matter that is raised by the ticket is a separate, but related, aspect of the car accident. The ticket is given by the police and it is a minor criminal case unless you are charged with a serious driving offense, such as driving under the influence of alcohol or drugs, reckless driving, or leaving the scene of an accident. The ticket will be handled in the usual way in traffic court.

If you get such a ticket, you will have to face the possibility of fines or points against your license, just as anyone else charged with a traffic offense. But, in addition to this, a ticket for you or the other driver may have significance in a civil case between you and the other driver. For this reason, you should be sure to advise your insurance company and lawyers who are representing you of the ticket and all facts pertaining to it, including the trial date.

CHAPTER 6

Buying a House

If you are like most people, buying a house will be the most expensive purchase you will ever make. In addition to this, buying a house affects your lifestyle in many ways. It establishes you in a neighborhood, it determines what sorts of activities are possible where you live, it affects your budget more than any other matter, and it says to others a good deal about the kind of life you are trying to live.

If you are buying a condominium or cooperative unit of some type, the procedures are essentially the same, even though those types of purchases are somewhat different, legally. Depending on the type of house you buy, the procedure may vary a little, but the differences will be obvious. For example, you do not need to worry about how to handle realtors if you find a house being sold by owner. If the house you are buying has public water and sewer, you obviously do not need to have a well or septic system inspected.

Checklist for Buying a House

- ❏ Determine your price range
- ❏ Determine what is absolutely necessary in your house
- ❏ Determine the locations that would be acceptable to you
- ❏ Select a realtor in the location where you are looking
- ❏ Verify real estate taxes, heating and utility costs, and other expenses
- ❏ Get a satisfactory sales contract
- ❏ Be sure that the seller endorses the insurance policy to cover you as an *additional insured* until closing
- ❏ Have the house properly inspected
- ❏ Obtain an acceptable financing commitment
- ❏ Be sure a title company is preparing for the closing
- ❏ Obtain homeowners insurance
- ❏ Participate in the closing
- ❏ Be sure real estate tax bills, utility bills, and all other house bills are in your name after closing

☑ Determine your price range

It is doubtful that you will ever get *everything* you want in a house. Big items, such as the number of rooms in the house, the general condition of the house, heating, and air conditioning, come first. Do not buy a house unless you can set a price range that will get you the major items you want in a house. As for smaller items, find out what it will cost to add them at a later time.

When you finally set your price range, do not kid yourself about the real cost of home ownership. At a minimum, you will be paying real estate taxes, insurance, repair and maintenance costs, utilities, grass cutting, possibly snow removal, and a number of incidental items. If you cannot afford $1,000 a month to spend on your house and you intend to finance it with a mortgage that has a $950 per month payment, you are living in la-la land.

☑ Determine what is absolutely necessary in your house

You have to distinguish between must have items and those that are not absolutely necessary. If you cannot live without air conditioning, it is a must have item. If you would like to have a washer and dryer upstairs, but can live with it in the basement, that item should not be a deal breaker. If you like everything about a house except a few things about the kitchen, do not pass it up simply for that reason.

When you select a realtor, you will want to furnish him or her with your must have list. This will avoid wasting your time and the realtor's on houses that could never be acceptable. Be sure that your must have list is clear about the number of rooms and bathrooms you need and where they should be located.

☑ Determine the locations that would be acceptable to you

The best way to be sure that a location works for you is to spend a little time in it. Try out your morning and evening commuting times during the rush hours. Try out the trips to the store and other places you go regularly. Talk with some of the neighbors to get a sense for what kind of neighborhood you are looking at. Be sure to visit the house at night as well as in the daytime. Neighborhoods and particular houses often feel different at night.

☑ Select a realtor in the location where you are looking

Unless you happen to find a house you want to buy from someone you know or by some other unusual break, you will be dealing with a realtor in buying a house. Buyers do not need to enter contracts with realtors and there is no need for you to do so. Realtors are paid by the seller on a commission basis (generally about six percent) and they receive no fee from the buyer. You want a realtor who is associated with a company that is active in the area where you are looking for your house.

You do not need to be in love with your realtor as long as he or she brings to your attention just about everything in the location and price range you are requesting. If you select a realtor who does not do this, get a new one. The relationship will be over as soon as you find your house. If you feel that you are not being shown houses that are available of the type and location you would like because of some personal characteristic such as your age, race, or religion, do something about it fast by contacting your state agency that handles such matters. This practice, which is in absolute violation of federal and state laws, is known as *steering*.

The buyer's realtor is paid by receiving part of the commission paid by the seller (generally one-half). In most states, a realtor can represent both a seller and a buyer of the same house if he or she gets a particular document signed by each of the parties. In most situations, this would be a conflict of interest that you should not agree to, but in the case of realtors, it is acceptable. In fact, realtors are usually at their most active when they are representing both the buyer and the seller of the same house, since then they receive the entire commission. Sometimes the realtor who lists the house is called the *listing agent* and the realtor who finds a buyer is called the *cooperating broker*. Do not spend time worrying about what the realtors call themselves or whether each is being paid sufficiently. In a residential house purchase, the fee is the seller's responsibility.

A good realtor will take care of a lot of the things you need to have done in order to buy a house. If your house has services that require verification in order for there to be a sale, for example, a yield test of a well to see that there is sufficient water when a house is not served by public pipes, a good realtor will arrange to get this done. A good realtor will also arrange for the termite inspection that is necessary and usually mandatory for a house to be sold. The termite inspection covers all forms of infestation, such as carpenter ants, in addition to termites. Most realtors will offer to arrange for an inspection of the house and they will generally recommend the inspector. It is probably better not to have your inspection done in this manner, as explained beginning on page 131.

One other item is important with regard to realtors. Since realtors only get paid when a house is sold, their first and foremost desire is to sell you one. Even the best realtor has a hard time bringing up matters that may halt the deal. It is up to you to insist upon things that are important to you and to ask the questions that will give you the information you need. Be as forceful about this as you need to be. Realtors are used to this and it does not bother them.

Verify real estate taxes, heating and utility costs, and other expenses

Almost every political subdivision in the United States imposes a real estate tax upon the transfer of real estate. In most instances, real estate taxes are imposed by counties (or cities that are not part of counties). In many areas, a large portion of the money that is collected through real estate taxes goes to public schools. What you need to know is how much you will be paying in real estate taxes and how often.

In most places in this country, real estate taxes on houses and other properties are adjusted every few years. Three years is a typical period of time for this. The period of time involved is sometimes called the *cycle*. You can determine what your real estate taxes will be for the remainder of a cycle and you can generally assume that unless there are substantial improvements or additions to your house, the next cycle will be somewhat higher (but not dramatically). You should be sure to verify the real estate taxes before you enter a contract to buy a house since your total cost of owning your house will include real estate taxes.

Although your realtor should do this work for you, the best way to be certain about the costs associated with a house is to look at the bills themselves. It is perfectly acceptable for a potential buyer to request a copy of the last tax bill and copies of the heating and utility bills for the past year. If there are any other expenses associated with a house you are thinking of buying, such as community association dues, they can be verified in the same fashion.

Remember that not every bill associated with a house is a monthly bill. Water bills, for example, are sometimes sent less frequently. Tax and insurance bills may be furnished biannually in some instances and sometimes at different time intervals. Be sure to compute all of the costs for a house you are considering on a monthly basis, whether they are billed that way or not. Unless you know your monthly cost for everything, you cannot determine whether a house is within your price range.

Get a satisfactory sales contract

This is a major item when you go to buy a house and a separate checklist is provided for it later in this chapter. Under no circumstances should you sign a sales contract or pay a deposit until the contract is completely satisfactory in all respects. Contracts are long-winded and boring, but take time to read it. If you do not understand something in a contract, ask someone about it. Since realtors deal with real estate contracts all the time, your realtor should be able to explain any provision of the contract to you. As you will see, a great deal of the contract is not negotiable or particularly important. The checklist about sales contracts will direct you to the points that are essential for you.

Be sure that the seller endorses the insurance policy to cover you as an additional insured until closing

Through a peculiarity of real estate law, the risk of loss or damage to real estate once it is under contract but before closing falls in most states upon the buyer. If you were to do nothing about this and if for some unforeseen reason damage to a house you had signed a contract to buy occurred, you would be responsible for the loss. There are two ways to address this matter. The easiest way is for there to be a provision in the sales contract stating that the risk of loss will be borne by the seller until closing. The other way to avoid it is for the seller's liability insurance policy to be endorsed to include the buyer as an *additional insured* until closing. Insurance companies generally charge nothing for such endorsements.

Have the house properly inspected

There are three general kinds of inspections that take place regarding houses—the building inspection, the infestation inspection, and the inspection of well and septic systems (if they are present). In some areas, it is customary for there to be a separate roof inspection and in others it is part of the building inspection. There are also an increasing number of areas in which radon tests have become standard.

Often, the seller will take care of the infestation inspection by obtaining what is known as a *termite certificate*. This is a certificate from a reputable company stating that the house is free of infestation by termites or other wood-boring insects. The seller should also obtain a radon certificate if that is customary in your area. In many states, well and septic inspections are required by state law and there are various companies licensed to provide them. Frequently, sellers will obtain these as well. The big item for you to take care of is the building inspection and possibly a separate roof inspection.

There are home inspection companies available everywhere and most of them have some connection with realtors. If you read the fine print about such companies, you would find that many of them belong to associations that actually state that the inspector is working for the realtor as well as the buyer. Since the realtor's only interest is in selling the house, whatever its condition, this is not good for you. The best building inspector for your purposes is a qualified builder who does not make a full-time job of inspecting houses for sale and is willing to go through the house for you to find out everything that is wrong with it. Builders who are busy generally do not want to spend their time doing this, but the incentive of getting work out of such a favor is often persuasive. If you can get a good builder who is properly licensed to do the inspection for you, that will certainly be to your benefit.

☑ Obtain an acceptable financing commitment

If you are like most people in the world, you will be buying your house with money coming from a mortgage. Most house loans come from savings and loan banks or finance companies. Ask your realtor to suggest a few in your area and compare them.

It is typical for people to borrow 80% of the purchase price of a house, and sometimes it is possible to borrow more than that. When more than 80% of the purchase price is borrowed, lenders generally require what is known as *mortgage guaranty insurance* or a *mortgage insurance premium*, because the risk for them is greater. In figuring out how much money you want to obtain by a mortgage, you must take into account the fact that you will be paying closing costs in addition to the rest of the purchase price. Realtors can compute what your closing costs will be quite accurately and you should get this done.

When you get a loan for a house, you are required to sign a document that gets filed with the land records in your state. In some states the document you are required to sign is known as a *mortgage* and in others as a *deed of trust*. Although there are some differences between mortgages and deeds of trust, they have no real significance for people borrowing money to buy a house. What is important to you are the terms of the loan you are getting. The title company will usually file the mortgage or deed of trust as well as your deed.

Loans to buy houses fall into two general categories. One of them is the *fixed rate* variety, which means exactly what it says. The interest rate is established at the beginning of the loan and remains unchanged for the whole term of the loan. The other is known as an *adjustable rate mortgage* (ARM). An ARM is a mortgage in which the interest rate is adjusted after a certain period of time, usually between one and five years, and possibly readjusted at a later time. When interest rates are low, a fixed-rate mortgage is most attractive. When you use an ARM-type mortgage, you take the risk of interest rates going up at the time the bank has the right to adjust the interest rate. Sometimes the bank is only allowed to adjust the interest rate by a certain amount (known as a *collar*), but whatever it is you take the risk.

Once you know how much money you will be borrowing, how long the loan will be, what the interest rate or rates will be, and your closing costs—including the money you need to put in escrow for real estate taxes and insurance, there is one other financial matter to consider. This is the matter of *points*.

Points are additional money that is charged by lenders for giving you a loan. Sometimes the cost of points is added to the loan itself and sometimes it is charged up front. Each point is equal to one percent of the amount you are borrowing. For a $150,000 loan, each point will cost $1,500. When mortgage money is tight, lenders tend to take advantage of that by charging points. The number of points they charge generally ranges from one-half point to three points, but other amounts are possible. When mortgage money is in great supply, and borrowers have more leverage, loans are sometimes made free of points. Your objective is to get the loan you want without paying any points or, if you have to pay points, paying as few as possible.

Loans for houses are of various lengths. Most of them are between fifteen and thirty years. The length of the loan is known as its *term*. If you are looking for the lowest possible monthly payments and are reasonably young, the longest possible term would probably be best for you. Since most mortgages permit you to prepay and refinance at any time (and a number of states require them to do this), you could always get a shorter term mortgage later or pay off the longer term mortgage earlier if you chose to do so. Remember, however, that there are always some costs connected with refinancing a house.

The mortgage or deed of trust you will need to sign in order to get a loan is a very complicated document. The good news is that these documents are always form documents that do not have controversial provisions in them. You will find that most lenders in your area use a document that virtually everyone signs with no questions at all.

The bank or finance company loan will require you to provide certain things in order for the loan to be made, but these are things you would want to have in any event. Almost all house loans require some forms of inspection, but as already discussed, you definitely want these in any event. These loans require you to have a homeowners insurance policy meeting certain standards, but you would certainly not want to own a home without such a policy.

Real estate lenders also require that you have title insurance. Title insurance guarantees that the deed giving ownership of the house to you does so with no qualifications except what are known as *customary easements* that pertain to every piece of property. These easements are things like the right of the power company to repair its wires on your property or the right of the water company to repair its pipes. Even if you did not have a mortgage, you would be very foolish not to obtain title insurance for yourself. If you have a mortgage, you should request the title company to provide owner's coverage as well as lender's coverage. This means that the title policy protects you as well as the bank or finance company. Fees for title policies are paid once at closing and their cost is quite reasonable.

When a bank loan is involved, the bank will generally arrange to have its attorneys prepare all of the closing documents. This is a load off your mind and you should let the bank worry about it. The bank's personnel do this every day. Unfortunately, all bank loans require the borrower to pay the lender's fee for this work. The fee is usually not large, but you should inquire about it.

Banks also require you to maintain what is known as an escrow account to keep money available for real estate taxes and homeowners insurance. In most instances, banks receive a monthly amount for those items, which is sufficient each year to pay for them. This is included in your monthly mortgage payment. Most banks pay for homeowners insurance and real estate taxes themselves, to be sure they are paid. The only thing you have to do is be sure the bills are sent to your bank when you receive them.

Be sure a title company is preparing for the closing

The buyer or lender will generally choose a title company to provide title insurance. A representative of that company will often be the person responsible for managing the closing (the *closing official*). It does not matter to you whether someone from the title company, the bank's attorney, or another individual does that job. You simply need to verify that a title company is preparing for the closing and that you and the lender will receive title insurance at the closing.

Obtain homeowners insurance

Homeowners insurance is a necessity for home ownership. In the first place, every lender in the world requires certain types of homeowners insurance as a condition of its loan. In the second place, since your house will almost surely be your most valuable asset, you definitely want it to be fully insured for all purposes. (A separate checklist for homeowners insurance is provided on p.149.)

 Participate in the closing

Closing is the time when you acquire ownership of your house and accept responsibility for it. Closings generally involve you, the seller, the realtor and someone from the title insurance company. There is a lot of paperwork at closings and some mathematics for you to follow as well. (A separate checklist for you to follow at your closing is provided on p.153.)

 Be sure real estate tax bills, utility bills, and all other house bills are in your name after closing

When the title company files your deed in the correct land records office, it will change the records pertaining to your house to be in your name. It is a good idea after a little while to check that this has occurred. If a tax bill or other state notice arrives in the name of the seller, that is a good indication that the records have not yet been changed. You should also advise the utility company that you are now the owner of the house, so that it can begin to send bills to you in your name. If there are other places, such as a community association, that communicate regularly with the owner of your house, advise those parties of the change in ownership.

Terms Used in Buying a House

- **additional insured.** The designation of a buyer when he or she is added to a seller's homeowners insurance policy.
- **adjustable rate mortgage (ARM).** A mortgage where the rate of interest changes from time to time.
- **building inspection.** An inspection of the structural, electrical, plumbing, and other aspects of a house by someone qualified to perform it.
- **closing (settlement).** The occasion at which final payments and transfer of property from seller to buyer takes place.
- **closing documents.** All the documents utilized in completing the purchase of a house.
- **covenants.** Assurances regarding title that are made in a deed.
- **deed.** The document that transfers ownership of property from one party to another.
- **deed of trust.** Another form of document that provides a lender with a security interest in the property.
- **documentary stamps.** Stamps reflecting evidence of payment of fees to counties or other political subdivisions for the transfer of real estate.
- **down payment.** The amount of money placed by a buyer in escrow and credited towards the purchase of a house.
- **escrow agent.** A person who holds a deposit until closing.
- **financing commitment.** A commitment by a lender to make financing for a house available under particular conditions for a certain amount of time.

- **fixed rate mortgage.** A mortgage where the rate of interest does not change.
- **fixtures.** Items that are attached to a house and sold with it.
- **homeowners insurance.** Insurance that protects lenders and owners from damage to property and from damage due to injuries to others.
- **HUD-1.** A federal form of settlement sheet that is widely used.
- **mortgage.** The document that provides a lender with a security interest in the property.
- **improvements.** Additions to the house or property that increase its value.
- **listing.** Placing a house for sale in a newspaper or other fashion.
- **listing agent.** A realtor who lists a house for sale.
- **mortgage guaranty insurance/mortgage insurance premium.** Repayment insurance required by the lender when more than 80% of the purchase price of a house is borrowed.
- **personal property.** Items included in a sale of real estate that are not part of the house.
- **points.** Charges imposed by lenders for providing loans (one point equals one percent of the amount borrowed).
- **premium.** The cost of a homeowner's or other insurance policy.
- **real estate contract.** The document that sets forth the terms of a sale of property from a seller to a buyer.
- **real estate taxes.** The taxes charged by counties or other political subdivisions for ownership of real estate.
- **realtor.** A person who sells houses for a commission.

- **recordable form.** A document which is suitable for recording in the public land records.
- **repairs.** Incidental work to maintain the house and the systems in it in working order.
- **settlement sheet.** The document that contains the mathematics respecting who pays what at a real estate closing.
- **tax cycle.** The number of years between re-evaluations of property for tax purposes.
- **termite certificate.** A document provided by a licensed pest control inspector stating that a house is free of termites and other infestation.
- **title.** Ownership to property.
- **title insurance.** Insurance that provides owners and lenders with protection in the event of a defect in title.
- **well yield test.** A test to determine the amount of water per minute available in a well.

• • • • •

Contract to Buy a House

If one or more realtors are involved in the deal, the contract you will be given will be a form contract of one of the realty companies. With a few variations, most of these contracts are fine for this purpose. If there is no realtor involved, you can buy a simple real estate purchase contract for houses at various stores that sell stationery products. You can use a lawyer if you want, but you are not required to do so.

Before turning to the specifics of contracts to buy houses, there are two basic rules you should know. First, real estate cannot be sold without a written contract. Therefore, until you have a written contract, signed by the seller (both husband and wife if that is how the house is owned) and by you, you do not have a deal.

Second, once you and the seller sign a contract, it is the entire deal. Representations that have been made to you by the seller, a realtor, or someone else are not part of the deal even if you were told otherwise. If the seller tells you there is a ten-year warranty on the roof, you have nothing to rely on for that statement unless you receive a copy of the warranty. The contract must state all of your rights until closing when you will receive a deed that gives the house to you. If you want the right to enter the house before closing, get it in the contract. If you want the right to bring an inspector in the house, get it in the contract.

Checklist for Contract to Buy a House

- ❑ Verify that the description of the house and property is correct
- ❑ Verify the purchase price and be sure that the deposit is credited
- ❑ Verify that the seller will pay the realtor
- ❑ Verify that you and the seller will split transfer costs
- ❑ Verify that real estate taxes will be apportioned as of the closing date
- ❑ Check that there is a provision requiring the seller to endorse the homeowners insurance policy to cover you until closing
- ❑ Be sure the closing date, time, and place are acceptable to you
- ❑ Be sure there is a suitable building inspection condition
- ❑ Be sure there is a suitable termite and other infestation condition
- ❑ Be sure the contract provides for well and septic inspection if necessary

- ❏ Be sure there is an appropriate financing condition in the contract
- ❏ Be sure the contract says that you will receive a deed at closing in recordable form, providing a special warranty or covenants against grantor's acts
- ❏ Be sure the contract says that the house will be delivered to you broom clean, with all keys, instruction manuals, warranties, plans, and other materials pertaining to the house
- ❏ Be sure everything that is to be sold with the house is covered in the contract
- ❏ Be sure the contract states that the deposit will be returned to you if the sale does not go through
- ❏ Be sure the contract affords you and your workers right of access to the house before closing if you want to have it
- ❏ Be sure the contract says that your title will be good and merchantable and insurable by major title insurance companies

☑ Verify that the description of the house and property is correct

Although it may seem silly, anyone buying a house should be sure that the house described in the contract is the correct house. If there are outbuildings, such as a garage or storage shed, be sure they are included. If there is any question about the boundaries of the property the house is situated on, get the seller or realtor to show you the survey and the survey marks on the property. Occasionally, people are disappointed by buying property that does not have the boundaries they thought they were getting.

Verify the purchase price and be sure that the deposit is credited

Your contract must state precisely what you are paying for the house. It should say that the deposit, which normally will not exceed 5%, will be held in *escrow* by an agreed person and credited to the purchase price at closing. Deposits will usually be held in escrow by one of the lawyers or the title company.

 Verify that the seller will pay the realtor

If there is a realtor, it is the seller's obligation to pay him or her. Since realtors get paid at closing, the one place you can be sure to find your realtor is at the closing table. If you have used your own realtor, he or she will be paid a portion of the fee received by the seller's realtor, usually one-half. This should also be provided in the contract. If there are no realtors, the contract should state that there have been none and that you will not be responsible if a realtor claims that he or she has dealt with the seller and is entitled to a commission.

 Verify that you and the seller will split transfer costs

Transfer costs may involve recording fees, documentary stamps, and other costs imposed by various counties to record real estate transfers. There is a custom almost everywhere that such costs are divided equally between buyers and sellers.

 Verify that real estate taxes will be apportioned as of the closing date

Each party to a real estate contract should be responsible for real estate taxes attributable to the time in which he or she owned the house. Since real estate taxes are normally imposed once a year (and frequently the tax year differs from the annual year), it is very unlikely that you will be closing just as a tax period ends. Therefore, the real estate contract should divide the real estate taxes between the parties in accordance with their periods of ownership. For example, if you live in a state where real estate taxes are imposed on a tax year of July 1–June 30 and you close on November 1, with the real estate taxes for the year already having been paid by the seller, you would be required to reimburse the seller for two-thirds (eight months out of twelve months) of those real estate taxes.

Check that there is a provision requiring the seller to endorse the homeowners insurance policy to cover you until closing

The need for this provision has already been explained. (see page 131.) You definitely want either the contract to say that the seller bears the risk of loss until closing or that the seller will endorse his or her insurance policy to cover you until closing. If the latter of these two solutions occurs, obtain a copy of the notice from the insurance company that there is such coverage. Insurance companies generally do not charge a fee for such endorsements.

Be sure the closing date, time, and place are acceptable to you

Closings generally take place at either the title company or another designated office and dates and times are negotiable. A lot of contracts say that closing will take place no later than a particular date and that is satisfactory provided the specific date and time are later agreed upon.

Be sure that there is a suitable building inspection condition

It is important that the contract indicates that it is conditioned on a building inspection taking place. There must also be a reasonable amount of time permitted for the inspection. Different contracts have different provisions about what occurs if the inspection finds defects in the house. Some contracts give the seller the right to fix defects up to a certain amount and give the buyer the right to void the contract if the repairs are not satisfactorily made.

This sort of provision is generally acceptable, but it is not the absolutely best provision for a buyer. The best provision for a buyer is one that says that the building inspection must be satisfactory to the buyer in his or her sole discretion and, if not, the buyer may void the contract. If you are able to get such a provision, you may still negotiate with the seller over small repairs if you want to do so. But if something is discovered that you simply do not want to have in your house, you can get out of the contract.

 Be sure there is a suitable termite and other infestation condition

This provision is found in virtually every standard real estate contract. As a general rule, the seller pays the cost of these inspections and provides a certificate from a licensed company stating that the house is free of termite or other insect infestation. If the inspector finds active infestation, treatment and possibly replacement of parts of the house structure may be required. If the inspection finds past infestation that has been treated, the question is whether that infestation has been eliminated without structural damage. If not, treatment with a suitable guarantee or repairs made at the seller's expense should be required before closing.

 Be sure the contract provides for well and septic inspection if necessary

If you have public water and sewer, these inspections are obviously not necessary. If not, state law generally requires that there be such inspections and, even if it does not, you absolutely want the contract to require them. Like the other inspection provisions, this provision should entitle you to void the contract if the results are not satisfactory.

With regard to well water, a buyer must be certain of both sufficient quantity and quality. Quantity is determined by what is known as a *well yield* test. This test tells you how many gallons per minute are available at the depth the well pump is working. State laws set minimums for this purpose and it is generally a good idea to have a well yield substantially in excess of that required by state law. Well yields tend to decrease during times of drought. With regard to quality, well water must be examined by a public or private laboratory certified for such purpose. Those laboratories are familiar with the required tests for well water and they will provide written reports.

Be sure there is an appropriate financing condition in the contract

In general, financing conditions in sales contracts state that the buyer will, within a short time following signing the contract (five or ten days is typical), apply for financing at one or more reputable lending institutions. The contract normally specifies the financing that will be applied for, such as a 30-year mortgage in the amount of $150,000 at a fixed interest rate not to exceed 6.5% per annum. Your contract should definitely state that you may accept financing on other terms if you wish to do so. Normally, real estate contracts say that the buyer will notify the seller as soon as the lending institution has made its decision.

Be sure the contract says that you will receive a deed at closing in recordable form, providing a special warranty or covenants against grantor's acts

The purpose of these words is that the seller promises the buyer that he or she has done nothing while he or she owned the house to invalidate the title. When you receive such a deed, you are protected in the event something like that were to occur in the future. Your title insurance will also provide you with protection in the event of any defects in the title.

 Be sure the contract says that the house will be delivered to you broom clean, with all keys, instruction manuals, warranties, plans, and other materials pertaining to the house

The purpose of the broom-clean provision is to assure that the buyer will not have to spend money removing items from the house that belong to the seller.

NOTE: *Be certain to get as many materials about your house from the previous owner as you can. Such things as plans and warranties on items in the house often turn out to be useful.*

 Be sure everything that is to be sold with the house is covered in the contract

Real estate contracts have general provisions indicating that things like kitchen appliances, washers and dryers, and other items are a part of the sale. There are questions, however, regarding things like air conditioners, window treatments, and sometimes lighting fixtures. Go through every room of the house carefully and be certain that the provision about additional property in the real estate contract includes everything you intend to get. As a general rule, things attached to the house, which are known as *fixtures*, go to the buyer unless otherwise specified.

✓ Be sure the contract states that the deposit will be returned to you if the sale does not go through

Most form real estate contracts have a provision to this effect, but you want to be certain of it for obvious reasons. Various states have laws regarding how deposits are to be treated.

✓ Be sure the contract affords you and your workers right of access to the house before closing if you want to have it

If you intend to do certain things to the house as soon as you buy it and need to have contractors or architects or other people get into the house to prepare for that, get a provision indicating that such people will be permitted to enter the house at reasonable times and with notice prior to closing.

✓ Be sure the contract says that your title will be good and merchantable and insurable by major title insurance companies

This is a form provision that your lender and the title company will want to see. If you have any questions whether provisions concerning the deed and title are satisfactory, ask the lender and the title company representative to look them over for you.

• • • • •

Homeowners Insurance

If you own a house, condominium, or cooperative, you absolutely need homeowners insurance. A lender will require this in any event. Homeowners insurance protects you in two ways. It protects you if someone injures him- or herself on your property and makes a claim against you. It also protects you if your house is damaged because of a fire or other hazard such as dangerous weather.

If you are buying a house in a coastal or low-lying area, you should be aware that most homeowners insurance does not cover flood damage. The only generally available coverage for damage from floods is federal flood insurance. Limited amounts of this insurance, depending on where your house is located and when you get it, are available through the same insurance brokers that sell homeowners insurance. This is a must-have if your house is in such an area and any lender will insist upon it.

The cost of homeowners insurance is known as the *premium*. Premiums are generally payable either annually or semiannually. You should compare the cost of a few well-rated insurance companies, because companies' prices differ for the same coverage. A good independent broker should be able to give you various prices. You can also obtain prices from a number of companies by telephone or on the Internet.

Be sure to get a copy of your homeowners insurance policy. If you use a bank loan, you will need to have a copy at closing for the bank. Most banks or other lenders require that the homeowners insurance policy contain a provision stating that it cannot be canceled unless the lender receives a certain amount of notice. Insurance companies are used to this and have no problem with it.

Be sure that the amount of insurance you buy for your house itself is sufficient for any type of disaster. Remember that values of houses go up as time passes. Some insurance policies contain an inflation provision that raises the amount of insurance coverage each year as costs go up. Others do not contain such a provision and you should be sure to look at the insured value each year to decide whether it is sufficient. You should know the cost of homeowners insurance before you enter a contract to buy a house since the total cost of owning your house will include it. Some insurance companies reduce their premiums if your house is located near a fire hydrant or if you have a security system.

Checklist for Homeowners Insurance

- ❏ Verify the insurance requirements of your lender
- ❏ Select a competent independent insurance broker to get insurance coverage
- ❏ Instruct the insurance broker to provide homeowners insurance possibilities with highly-rated companies
- ❏ Buy a homeowners insurance policy that has an inception date the same as the planned date for your closing
- ❏ Be sure that your homeowners insurance policy includes a certain amount of coverage for losses out of your house
- ❏ Be sure that your homeowners insurance policy adequately covers loss of use compensation
- ❏ Obtain a copy of your homeowners insurance policy

☑ Verify the insurance requirements of your lender

The financial commitment of any lender will specify the insurance requirements you must satisfy. Homeowners are required to have an insurance policy meeting certain requirements in force at all times. The insurance policy will protect the interests of both the lender and you. The lender's commitment will specify the amounts of property damage and liability insurance required or it will state something about what constitutes acceptable limits of liability. All you need to do is show the requirements to an insurance broker and he or she will know exactly how to satisfy them.

☑ Select a competent independent insurance broker to get insurance coverage

As with every form of insurance, the selection of an independent broker, one not wedded to a particular company, is best. Such a broker can make comparisons of coverage and price and offer you various options. For homeowners insurance, there are always a number of high-quality insurance companies doing business in any particular market.

☑ Instruct the insurance broker to provide homeowners insurance possibilities with highly-rated companies

Insurance companies are rated by a number of national agencies, including *A.M. Best's*, *Moody's*, and *Standard and Poor's*. All insurance brokers have the ratings available to them and can advise you accordingly. Even if the premium is lower, do not buy homeowners insurance from poorly-rated companies.

☑ Buy a homeowners insurance policy that has an inception date that is the same as the planned date for your closing

You will need to provide a copy of your insurance policy and a copy of the paid receipt for the first year's premium at the time of your closing. You should get both of those items from your insurance broker when you buy the policy. Since you are not responsible for insurance until the closing date and since the lender will require you to have insurance effective on that date, the first year of your coverage should begin on the planned closing date.

Be sure that your homeowners insurance policy includes a certain amount of coverage for losses out of your house

These sorts of provisions are sometimes referred to as *floater* protection. Typically, floater protection is in a much smaller amount than general liability coverage, but it protects you against losses for a certain amount of your possessions outside your house.

 Be sure that your homeowners insurance policy adequately covers loss of use compensation

If a fire or other disaster were to make your house unusable and you needed to rent an apartment or hotel room for a period of time, this coverage would apply. The inclusion of this coverage in a homeowners insurance policy is not generally required by lenders, but it is also not usually very expensive. It is worth having because, in the event of a disaster, the last thing you need is to have to continue paying all of your homeowner's expenses as well as the cost of living somewhere else.

 Obtain a copy of your homeowners insurance policy

For some reason many people do not have copies of their own insurance policies. This is a very bad idea since your policies not only tell you what is covered, but also how to proceed if you have to make a claim. Most insurance policies state specific procedures for making a claim and, if you do not follow them, it is possible to lose your claim.

● ● ● ● ●

Closing

Closing is the time when you acquire ownership of your house. It is sometimes referred to as *settlement*. If you obtain a loan, the bank or

other lender will generally arrange the closing. Closing cannot take place until everything is done with regard to your loan. This means:
- all inspections have been completed;
- all price adjustments that are necessary have been agreed upon;
- real estate taxes have been verified;
- homeowners insurance has been purchased;
- a termite certificate has been issued;
- title insurance has been obtained;
- the deed and other necessary documents have been prepared; and,
- any other matters required by your state or by the lender have been accomplished.

At closing, the bank's representative will be certain to get the things the bank needs for the occasion. In addition, whoever is conducting the closing, often the title company representative, will request the things he or she requires. From your point of view only three items have particular importance. Those items are the Deed, the Mortgage (or Deed of Trust), and the Settlement Sheet. The first two items will be filed with the land records office that applies to your area and a copy of the Settlement Sheet will be provided to you to confirm the computation pertaining to payments.

Checklist for House Closing

- ❑ Be sure that someone has done a *walk-through* of the house to verify that everything required has been left in it and it is broom clean
- ❑ Receive a copy of your Deed and be sure the original is being correctly filed
- ❑ Be sure the Settlement Sheet is correct and that you receive a copy of it
- ❑ Read and sign all forms you are required to sign
- ❑ Be sure whoever is holding your deposit pays it to the closing official
- ❑ Pay the amount of money you owe including all of your costs after deducting financing and deposit
- ❑ Receive copies of every document used at closing
- ❑ Receive all keys, plans, instruction manuals, warranty materials, and other materials regarding the house and its contents

✓ Be sure that someone has done a *walk-through* of the house to verify that everything required has been left in it and it is broom clean

The last look at a house to see that everything is right for closing is known as a *walk-through*. Before you go to closing, you or your realtor if you are using one, should inspect the house to be sure that everything you agreed would be left in it has been left and its condition is what it is supposed to be. The house should be delivered *broom clean*, which means that it should be free of any possessions that should have been removed from it.

Receive a copy of your Deed and be sure the original is being correctly filed

The Deed is the document giving you title or ownership to your house. The original Deed is signed by the seller (both husband and wife if that is how the house is owned) and filed in the proper land records by the title company's representative. You will receive the original Deed after it is filed in the state land records. In the meantime, you should leave closing with a copy of your Deed for your records. (If you are buying a cooperative, you will not receive a Deed. You will receive a stock certificate for your shares in the cooperative and a proprietary lease for the unit you will be occupying.) No ordinary person can make any sense out of the descriptions and historical statements in a Deed. The only things you need to check are that your house has been properly identified and that you (both parties if there are two parties) are the person being granted the property.

 Be sure the Settlement Sheet is correct and that you receive a copy of it

The Settlement Sheet is the mathematical determination of who owes how much money for different things. Generally, the real estate taxes are divided between seller and buyer based upon the date of closing and all required transfer taxes and costs (in some states these include what are known as documentary stamps) necessary for filing are divided equally between seller and buyer. The cost of title insurance, covering both the lender and you, is paid for by you. You are also required to pay any open costs for any of the inspections and, if you have not already done so, for the homeowners insurance policy.

    The type of Settlement Sheet used most often is a *HUD-1 federal form* that lists separately the costs that are paid by the seller and by the buyer. This is a two-page form and the title company representative who conducts the closing will generally run through it out loud, item by item. Whether he or she does this or not, ask questions until you are completely satisfied with the mathematics leading up to the amount you owe. You will be paying the amount of the purchase price that is not covered by your loan as well as your share of the closing costs. The deposit you paid when you entered the sales contract will be deducted from what you owe. Usually the deposit is held in the escrow account of one of the realtors. You should be sure to leave the closing with a copy of the Settlement Sheet.

Read and sign all forms you are required to sign

A number of other forms required at closing are simply to comply with the federal government's rules for its insured banks. You will have to verify such things as where you live, where the money came from, and some other items. These are very simple matters and you should simply sign the necessary forms to verify the true statements that are on them. For completeness, you should also receive copies of each of these forms at closing.

The title company representative may not have a copy of the title policy, but he or she will give you a verification sheet if you ask for it. Since you want to be sure that title insurance covers you as well as the bank, obtain a copy of this as well.

Be sure whoever is holding your deposit pays it to the closing official

It is not likely that the closing official will overlook this item, but you should be certain it is accomplished nevertheless. There will not be sufficient funds for closing unless the deposit is paid to the closing official. If a realtor has been involved, that person will be at the closing table with a broad smile on his or her face. Be sure that person gets paid out of the seller's funds, since you will hear about it for the rest of your life if that does not happen.

 Pay the amount of money you owe including all of your costs after deducting financing and deposit

Check all the mathematics to your heart's content before you do this. Have the closing official be certain that he or she has accounted for every item. You will be charged for initial deposits for taxes and insurance in the escrow account. Get all of this straight with the closing official no matter how long it takes. The closing official will let you know how much you will be billed monthly for the escrow account as well as your mortgage payment.

 Receive copies of every document used at closing

You should leave closing with copies of every document that was used in it. In addition to the above mentioned documents, be sure you leave with copies of the Deed and Mortgage (or Deed of Trust). The closing official or someone at the title company will be responsible for filing the originals of these documents in the land records.

The whole group of documents are known as your *closing documents*. Keep them in a separate folder in a secure place in case you ever need to refer to them. Although there are a lot of details taken care of at closings, you cannot go wrong if a properly signed Deed was given to the title company official (he or she will be sure that it is in proper form) and the Settlement Sheet is correct about the amount you must pay. Since you have taken care of all the inspections, homeowners insurance, title insurance, and real estate taxes, there are no other big items you may have overlooked.

Receive all keys, plans, instruction manuals, warranty materials, and other materials regarding the house and its contents

It is important that you receive all of these items at closing. If the seller has forgotten to bring any such items to closing, make arrangements to get them immediately or you will probably never see them. It is a good precaution to get the tumblers of the door locks changed when you buy a house.

• • • • •

Repairs and Improvements to Your House

For legal purposes, there are two types of expenses in connection with the condition of houses. One type of expense is repairs and routine maintenance. The other type of repairs is known as *improvements* or *capital improvements*. These are items attached to the house or property in a permanent way. You can obtain a list of possible improvements from any accountant or tax preparer.

There are three reasons why you must keep a record of all improvements to your house. The first is a tax reason. If you sell your house in the future, and make a profit doing so, the amount of that profit for tax purposes depends upon what is known as your *basis*. Your basis is the amount you paid for the house including the cost of capital improvements. You cannot prove that amount accurately unless you have sufficient records. Since you want the basis to be as high as legally possible, you want to be sure that you are able to prove the cost of all improvements. You may not need to pay tax on any profits on such a sale for a variety of reasons, such as reinvestment in another principal residence or certain tax exemptions, but while you are living in your house there is no certainty what the tax laws might be when you sell it. If you have all of your records of costs for improvements, you will be covered in any event.

The second reason for keeping such records is that you can sometimes use them to get a higher price someday when you sell your house. For example, if you can prove that you put new plumbing in the house within the last few years and it cost a certain amount, a buyer might find the house to be more valuable.

Lastly, it is always a good idea to keep records on hand in case you have to have any future dealings with contractors or suppliers concerning the improvements. This could include issues regarding workmanship, covered repairs, or simply information of what was done to make further improvement easier. If you have a complete record of all improvements, you will be prepared to prove these things at any time in the future.

Section III

The Essentials

Insurance and Medical Care

CHAPTER 7

Liability Insurance

The first rule about buying insurance is simple—you buy insurance to cover risks you cannot afford to take. If you can take a risk, take it and save your money for something else. People who buy collision insurance for cars that are ready for the junkyard are throwing away their money. People who buy life insurance for young children who support nobody are doing the same thing. Since insurance is the only purchase you will ever make that you hope you will not use, the idea is to spend the least money possible to cover risks that are simply too great to bear.

On the other hand, insurance is an absolute necessity for risks that could destroy you financially. You simply must have adequate medical insurance even if your health is perfect and everyone in your family has lived to age 90. Anyone can experience a serious illness or injury at any time and very few people have anything close to the amount of money medical care for such an experience would cost.

The same is true for liability insurance of different kinds. You need sufficient automobile insurance whether your state requires it or not. If you hit a healthy 38-year-old neurosurgeon with three children, you probably will not earn enough money in your life to pay for the accident. If someone slips and falls in your apartment and puts out an eye on the end of one of your tables, you will not escape legal responsibility for the injury because you are paying only $400 a month rent.

In addition to insurance that everyone needs, there are types of insurance that particular people require because of their personal situation. For example, if you make your living with special tools, playing a musical instrument, or taking photographs with an expensive camera, you would be very foolish not to insure those items sufficiently. If you make your living driving your own truck that carries expensive materials or doing work in other people's homes, the risks you cannot take are obvious and must be properly insured. The point is that you must consider your own situation as well as the general risks that nearly all people face.

Your first responsibility with regard to insurance is figuring out what you need and what you do not need. Since each type of insurance is sold in different forms of insurance policies, you should begin by simply deciding what types of insurance are necessary for you. As I stated, you need medical insurance and certain forms of liability insurance no matter what your personal situation may be. If you own an automobile or rent an apartment, specific forms of liability insurance are necessary. Disability insurance is very useful, but it is also very expensive. (Most people do not get disability insurance unless their employer provides it.)

Special forms of insurance may be necessary for you because of your particular work or particular risks that occur in your life. Once you have thought about the matter carefully and decided what types of insurance are necessary for you, the next question is the best way to buy the insurance you need.

Many forms of liability insurance are part of the insurance policies you acquire for special purposes. For example, liability insurance is a main feature of automobile insurance. Liability insurance is also a part of renter's (or apartment) insurance and homeowners insurance as well. These matters are discussed more fully in the respective chapters dealing with those subjects.

The general idea behind liability insurance is that it covers you if you injure someone else or someone else's property through carelessness, which is known in legal terms as *negligence*. If you hit someone with your car, your car insurance covers that matter. If someone is injured in your apartment or house, your apartment or homeowners insurance comes into play. Depending upon the things you do that present a risk to other people or their property, you may need additional forms of liability insurance. For example, if you have a store, you need liability insurance to cover you if someone is hurt in your store. If you are a contractor, you need liability insurance to protect you against the risk that you may hurt another person or damage their property.

You will need to discuss these special kinds of liability insurance with a knowledgeable insurance broker if you engage in such activities, but there are certain basic things you should know about liability insurance in any event.

Checklist for Obtaining Liability Insurance

❏ Consider additional coverage for risky matters that are not covered by your existing automobile, apartment, or homeowners insurance policies
❏ Determine whether your employer or another party provides sufficient liability coverage for your work
❏ Familiarize yourself with limitations on your liability insurance coverage
❏ Be sure that your liability insurance policies provide for adequate legal representation when necessary
❏ Be sure that your liability insurance companies are highly rated
❏ Be sure that the limits of liability are sufficient
❏ Consider whether umbrella insurance is appropriate
❏ Retain a complete copy of all liability insurance policies

☑ Consider additional coverage for risky matters that are not covered by your existing automobile, apartment, or homeowners insurance policies

If there is nothing about your life besides driving a car and renting or owning a place to live that presents any possibility of damage to other persons or property, you should not need liability insurance beyond your automobile and apartment or homeowner's policies. If the limits of liability of those policies are sufficiently high to protect you, the subject of additional liability insurance is closed. If not, and if you cannot get the limits raised for a reasonable additional fee, ask an insurance broker about *umbrella insurance*. Umbrella insurance is reasonably inexpensive and covers particular risks above the limit of the primary insurance policies.

☑ Determine whether your employer or another party provides sufficient liability coverage for your work

Employers generally carry liability insurance that covers their employees for things they do in their employment such as drive automobiles or trucks or work machinery. If your work involves regular hazards, such as those of a contractor, coverage of this nature is absolutely required. In some instances, such as where people do writing work for others, the party who pays for the work may provide insurance even though the worker is an independent contractor. Get this straight before you begin any work and if the insurance coverage is not sufficient do not accept the work.

If you are working for a company or another person or partnership, you need to consider how risks you are exposed to in your job are handled. If you an *independent contractor*—not an employee of someone else but does jobs for other people—you will be responsible for your own liability insurance. This is true for almost all tradesmen and for most professional workers such as doctors, lawyers, and accountants. If you have a full-time job for a company as its employee, you would normally be insured by liability insurance provided by your employer. For example, nurses who are employed by hospitals, electricians who work for power companies, and truck drivers who work for trucking companies are generally insured by their employers. This is something to be checked very carefully when you sign on for employment.

 Familiarize yourself with limitations on your liability insurance coverage

Liability insurance may not cover *intentional acts* or acts that are the result of what is known as *gross negligence*. An intentional act is something you do on purpose. Gross negligence is something you do out of recklessness. For example, if you were to intentionally drive your car into somebody, that would be an intentional act and may not be covered by your automobile insurance. If you were to drink to excess and drive your car down the road at ninety miles an hour and hit someone, the insurance company could argue that was reckless and, therefore, gross negligence.

Acts that present the possibility of harm to people or property are often unavoidable, and insurance is available to deal with them. Acts that purposely or recklessly endanger people or property are avoidable and insurance companies often say in their policies that they do not cover such acts. Therefore, do not engage in acts that intentionally inflict harm or are done in a reckless manner.

 Be sure that your liability insurance policies provide for adequate legal representation when necessary

One of the biggest advantages of liability insurance is that it covers the expense of your legal defense if you are sued for the kind of liability that is protected by a particular liability insurance policy. Since lawyers and other costs involved in lawsuits can be very high, this is important. In most instances, the insurance company selects the lawyer who defends you in such a case and makes most of the important determinations about how to handle the case. Many insurance policies give the insurance company the right to settle a case if it wants to do so. Others let people who buy insurance reject a settlement, but then hold them responsible for expenses above the settlement amount that was rejected.

You should assume that once you buy insurance to take care of particular liability risks, you are in the hands of the insurance company for nearly all purposes. Although this is sometimes a mixed blessing, no one who thinks about it carefully would fail to have liability insurance to take care of risks like driving, renting, owning a house, or working in an occupation that presents dangers.

 Be sure that your liability insurance companies are highly rated
As with all forms of insurance, liability insurance should be acquired from insurance companies that are highly rated. In certain areas, particularly automobile liability, state laws require certain amounts of liability insurance. Some states provide insurance companies that make automobile insurance available to people who cannot buy it elsewhere. (Automobile insurance is discussed in Chapter 5.)

 Be sure that the limits of liability are sufficient
The amount of liability insurance that is appropriate is an important consideration. Often buying more than the bare minimum coverage is recommended. For example, if you live in a state that requires a small amount of car insurance, say $20,000 per collision, it is a good idea to buy more insurance than that. As a general rule, additional liability insurance does not cost much more than minimum coverage and pro-

vides a good deal of extra protection. Claims for injuries today are often for very large amounts and you do not want to be exposed to them without adequate liability insurance.

☑ Consider whether umbrella insurance is appropriate

Although this is a form of insurance you almost certainly will not need early in your work life, it is worth knowing about. Umbrella insurance covers liabilities that are greater than those covered in basic insurance policies. For example, if you had an automobile insurance policy with a liability limit of $50,000 per collision and a homeowners insurance policy with a liability limit of $75,000, you could buy an umbrella insurance policy that would assure you more liability protection both for driving your car and having people in your house. Umbrella insurance comes into play when there are claims above the liability limits of the basic policies that are listed in it.

If you purchase umbrella insurance, you must be certain that it covers liabilities in the areas where you are facing risks and that the umbrella insurance policy takes over above the liability limits of your individual insurance policies. Unless you are facing some unusual risks, or are unable to buy basic liability policies with high enough limits, umbrella insurance is probably not sensible for you.

☑ Retain a complete copy of all liability insurance policies

As discussed with regards to life and disability insurance policies, always insist on a complete copy of your policy and keep it in a safe place.

CHAPTER 8

Medical Care

The decision to get medical insurance is a no-brainer. Even if your health is perfect and you do not do anything more dangerous than look out the window, illness or injury is always a possibility. The cost today of even a small number of doctor bills or a minor hospital visit can be very high. The cost of a lengthy illness or injury is gigantic.

Checklist of Types of Medical Insurance

- ❏ Traditional Indemnity Insurance
- ❏ Preferred Provider Insurance
- ❏ Point-of-Service Medical Insurance
- ❏ Medicare
- ❏ Health Maintenance Organizations (HMOs)

Traditional Indemnity Insurance

This form of medical insurance is almost unavailable today. When it is available, it is extremely expensive. With traditional indemnity insurance, you select your medical care providers and the insurance company agrees to pay reasonable fees for your necessary medical care. The insurance company may still argue that a particular service is unnecessary or that its cost is unreasonable. These insurance policies may also exclude or limit particular forms of service such as physical therapy or psychiatric care. Unless money is virtually unlimited, this form of medical insurance is not usually a wise choice.

 Preferred Provider Insurance

This is medical insurance in which the insurance company provides you with a list of medical care providers that have agreed to rates for particular services. With this form of medical insurance, you are free to select your medical care providers from this list. In some instances, the list of approved medical care providers is extensive and of high quality. In other instances, this is not the case. If you select this form of medical insurance, you must be sure that the hospitals, physicians, and others you will want to use for your medical care are on the insurance company's list. You should also be sure you understand how you go about getting specialized forms of medical care, what care is excluded from coverage, how much of your medical bills you must pay (*co-pay*), and how much you must spend on medical care before your insurance takes over (*deductible*).

 Point-of-Service Medical Insurance

This is a form of medical insurance in which you must obtain your medical care at one or more fixed locations. This form of medical insurance obviously limits your choice of medical care providers. Since the locations that are designated in point-of-service medical insurance do not provide all medical services, you must be sure if you obtain this kind of medical insurance that you understand how other forms of medical care will be provided if you need them. Point-of-service medical insurance is not a good choice for you unless the designated location or locations are well-equipped to handle most of your medical care needs.

 Medicare

Medicare is one of the *Federal Insurance Contributions Act* (FICA) benefits for which deductions are taken from your paycheck. When you reach retirement age, which is between 65 and 67, or if you become disabled sooner, you become eligible for Medicare. Part A of Medicare, the hospital insurance part, is automatically provided. Part B of Medicare, the medical insurance part, is available for an additional fee, which is currently $66.60 per month. When you become eligible for Medicare, you will want to consider Medicare Supplement Insurance to make up the difference for the low payments Medicare makes to medical care providers. You will also want to learn about Medicare HMOs. These are HMOs that are available as a substitute for Medicare in certain places.

Health Maintenance Organizations (HMOs)

Most people today wind up getting medical insurance in the form of membership in a health maintenance organization (HMO). If your employer or the employer of your spouse or domestic partner provides its employees with the opportunity to participate in a particular health insurer, generally an HMO, that is almost certainly the way to go. Some employers pay a portion of the monthly expense of medical insurance and a few pay the whole cost. If your employer pays even part of the cost of your membership, that is one very good reason to join the medical plan it makes available. Another good reason is that members of groups generally have more leverage with health insurers, including HMOs, than individual members. This is because health insurers make more money on group memberships and do not want to risk losing them by having dissatisfied members.

HMOs are organizations in which members pay a fee in return for receiving access to medical service providers ranging from full-service hospitals to individual physicians as well as drugs, medical supplies, and everything else that relates to medical care. HMOs differ widely in the quality and quantity of medical services they provide to members.

When you belong to an HMO, you are assigned a general or *primary care* physician who provides the gateway to all of your medical care. In fact, this physician is sometimes known as a *gatekeeper*. You are known as a *member* or *covered person*. Your general physician determines what medical care you need, when you should be referred to a specialist, what testing should be done, what drugs should be prescribed, what forms of therapy you need, and many other matters essential to your medical care. Some HMOs permit you to choose from extensive lists of general physicians and others have very restricted lists that may not include the best physicians in your area. Since *gatekeeper* physicians may receive direct or indirect incentives to save money by limiting your medical services and even by failing to provide you with information about your medical options, the integrity of your general physician is terribly important to you.

Members of HMOs have no say about the fees that are paid to their medical care providers. Medical care providers are paid by HMOs on a salary, a *fee-for-service* basis, or what is known as a *capitation* basis. Payment on a fee-for-service basis means what it says, a fee at an agreed rate for each service. Payment on a capitation basis means that the medical care provider, generally a physician, is paid a fixed fee for providing all medical services of a particular type to a large number of members. Low fees to medical care providers and particularly capitation fees are unfavorable for people who have HMO medical insurance because your physician does not have a financial incentive to go the extra mile for you. Since physicians and other medical care providers are not required to participate in any HMO, the HMOs that pay better fees generally have higher quality lists of physicians.

As with any form of medical insurance, your contract with your HMO is the basic document stating your right to receive medical care. This means that when you belong to an HMO you have agreed to the terms and conditions of the contract between you and the HMO. If that contract says you are responsible for a particular portion of fees or that you will not be entitled to particular services, you must live with those costs or limitations. Since it is difficult for people to choose the best HMO, things you should consider are listed in the next section. If you have no choice about which HMO to use because your employer has selected an HMO for employees and will pay part of the cost, you will not be able to make a selection. If you are married and both of you are working, you may have two possibilities from which to choose. Be sure that whatever coverage you get includes coverage for your spouse if you are married and, of course, any children.

Do not approach the selection process assuming that everything about all HMOs is contrary to your medical care interests. Even though there are controversies all the time about what services are paid for and the ways gatekeeper physicians are used, it is not correct that everything about HMOs is bad. If you discuss HMOs with a lot of people who are covered by them, the picture that emerges is that there are great differences in the satisfaction people have with their HMOs. There are also great differences in the way physicians feel about different HMOs. Most of the time the HMOs that get good grades from physicians also get good grades from members.

Selecting an HMO

If you determine that your and your spouse's or domestic partner's employer does not provide satisfactory medical services, the next step for you is to obtain an independent insurance broker. Choose a broker who is a member of the *National Association of Health Underwriters* or a related state association, since he or she will be able to provide you with numerous possibilities for choosing an HMO. You do not want to select a broker or agent who is wedded to a particular company.

Bear in mind as you list the HMOs that are possibilities for you that state laws often provide that HMOs and other medical insurers must accept various groups of people. Of course, discrimination on the basis of race, creed, color, religion, sex, and some other factors is absolutely prohibited by federal and state laws. There are also laws that require medical insurers to accept people in certain occupations and other situations. This is something you can learn from your state office or a good independent broker. You should make your selection from every reasonable possibility.

There are many things for you to consider in selecting the best HMO. Depending on your circumstances and the HMOs that do business in your state, you may have a few or you may have many choices. Some HMOs have several different programs from which you may select. There is no simple way to select the best HMO and the best program for you, but there are factors that will lead you to that decision. Use the information you are able to acquire from your independent broker, your friends and relatives, your doctors, and any other sources to get the information about each of these factors. When you find it necessary to do so, call an HMO you are considering and ask questions until you receive the information you need.

Terms Used in HMO Provider Agreements

- **approval.** Agreement by an HMO to pay for medical services.
- **approved provider.** A medical care provider on an HMO's regular roster.
- **co-pay.** The amount you must pay for a medical service in addition to the amount the HMO pays.
- **coverage.** The medical care provided by an HMO.
- **deductible.** The amount of money a member must pay before the HMO begins paying.
- **HMO.** Health Maintenance Organization.
- **limit of liability.** The maximum financial responsibility of an HMO.
- **member (covered person).** A person who belongs to an HMO.
- **off-line provider.** A medical care provider not on an HMO's regular roster.
- **pre-approval.** Agreement to pay by an HMO before services are provided.
- **primary care physician (gatekeeper).** The general physician assigned to a member of an HMO.
- **provider.** A person or business who provides medical care.
- **referral.** A general physician's authorization for a member to see a specialist.

Checklist of Factors to Consider in Selecting an HMO

- ☐ Cost
- ☐ Quality of medical care providers
- ☐ Coverage for preexisting illnesses and injuries
- ☐ Level of service
- ☐ Preventive and emergency services
- ☐ Drug programs
- ☐ Dispute resolution
- ☐ Physician preferences
- ☐ Other sources of information
- ☐ History in your state
- ☐ Financial strength and affiliation
- ☐ National Committee for Quality Assurance ratings and accreditation
- ☐ Other national ratings

 Cost

Payment for medical insurance, including HMOs, is generally required monthly. Most contracts for medical insurance today do not extend for more than one year and most medical insurance costs increase significantly each year. Your basic monthly charge generally depends upon whether you are a single individual, a married individual covering your spouse and any children, or a single individual with children. Some medical insurance plans in some states cover significant others besides spouses. If your employer is paying some or all of your medical insurance costs, it is important for you to determine how much of that cost you are responsible for paying.

The cost to you of a particular HMO is not determined simply by the monthly charge for your coverage and the amount, if any, your employer is paying. Two other costs must be taken into account.

First, you must determine whether you are required to pay any cost before the HMO takes over (your deductible). Some deductibles are a single amount of money each year and some are an amount of money for each person who is covered per year. If this is the case, it is possible that you, your spouse, and each of your children could be required to pay a certain amount of money for medical care each year. You must also determine whether an HMO requires members to pay a portion (usually a relatively small amount) of the cost of each service (a *co-pay*). Depending upon the amount and the number of times you must pay it, this cost may become significant in determining your overall cost.

Second, the cost of any medical insurance requires you to take into account medical services you or other members of your family may require that are not covered. If your HMO does not cover the medical care costs of an illness or injury you suffered before you became covered (a *preexisting illness or injury*), the cost of treatment for that illness or injury must be taken into account by you. Since HMOs, like other medical insurers, sometimes argue that a new illness is really a preexisting illness because it came about due to a preexisting illness, you must be very careful about the possibility of such exclusions. It is preferable whenever possible to purchase HMO or other forms of medical insurance without preexisting illness or injury exclusions.

In addition, some HMOs do not provide coverage for particular services that are identified in the contracts. For example, psychiatric or psychological services, physical therapy (sometimes above a certain number of treatments per year), home medical care of different sorts, and experimental therapies are often excluded from coverage. Depending upon your particular circumstances, such exclusions may concern you. It is important for you to understand what services are excluded or limited in order for you to understand the costs of different HMOs.

A simple way of determining the cost of an HMO is as follows.

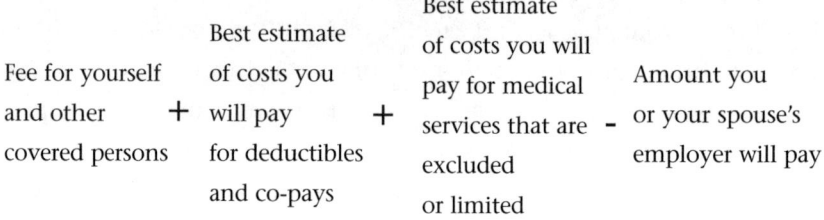

Cost of HMO = Fee for yourself and other covered persons + Best estimate of costs you will pay for deductibles and co-pays + Best estimate of costs you will pay for medical services that are excluded or limited − Amount you or your spouse's employer will pay

As you can see, there may be times when your cost for medical care will be lower even though the monthly fee of a particular HMO is higher. Reasonable additional monthly charges are almost always worth it if they permit you to get rid of preexisting illness and injury exclusions or enlarge the range of covered services that you or a member of your family may require.

☑ Quality of medical care providers

Since HMOs provide members with medical care from a group of approved providers, it is essential that you evaluate the list of providers of each HMO you are considering. These lists change from time to time and they are available from each of the HMOs. The lists include the general or primary care physicians available to you (gatekeepers), the specialists in each specific field, the hospitals, the testing facilities, and the other providers of medical care. The lists of approved providers of HMOs differ greatly in quantity and quality. You may also find that a general practitioner you and your family have long relied upon is available in certain HMOs and not available in others.

You should review the medical care providers approved by each HMO you are considering in several ways. Review the lists to determine whether physicians you have relied upon, including general practitioners and specialists, are on them. Review the lists to determine whether a good selection of specialists is available in fields you are likely to need in the future. If you or a member of your family has had a need in recent years for particular forms of specialized care, you should be particularly interested in the providers the HMOs you are considering have approved for that purpose.

A good selection of hospitals is also important. If the best hospitals for your care in the vicinity where you live are not on an HMO's list of approved providers, that is obviously a matter of concern to you.

As is the case with each of the factors you will be considering in selecting an HMO, the matter of approved medical care providers is something you should not be reluctant to ask questions about. If an HMO does not want to clearly advise you what medical care providers it is presently approving in your area, you should make it clear to whomever you are dealing with that you cannot make an evaluation of that HMO. People who use a particular HMO almost always know a lot about the quality of its approved provider list.

✔ Coverage for preexisting illnesses and injuries

This is coverage for illnesses or injuries that began before the time you join an HMO. If you have such a condition, this is a matter to be checked very carefully. You should be certain that ongoing treatment, including drugs that you require, is covered as well as treatment for new occurrences in your condition.

Since HMOs may consider a condition to be preexisting if anything remotely related to it was present before you became a member, you must be very clear about this matter. In many instances you will be required to complete an application that includes questions about any preexisting illnesses or injuries.

☑ Level of service

The level of service provided to members of HMOs differs greatly. In some instances, the service an HMO provides is strong in one way, but deficient in another. The process of comparing the services of HMOs requires a hard look on your part. It may be useful for you to make a list of services that are of special interest to you. You should compare how the different HMOs you are considering provide those services. If you have ongoing medical needs, such as a permanent injury or chronic illness like diabetes that require regular medical assistance, you should look carefully at how each HMO deals with those conditions.

It is important to understand how each HMO you are considering will use your general or primary care physician with regard to referrals to other medical service providers. Some HMOs make it difficult for general physicians to refer their patients to specialists or for testing or other types of medical care. Some HMOs permit referrals to specialists without much difficulty, but limit the services that may be provided by the specialists once a member sees them. Some HMOs allow certain forms of testing without much difficulty once a referral has been made, but limit the general physician's testing authority. Many HMOs have specific rules regarding second opinions.

☑ Preventive and emergency services

HMOs differ widely on the approval of examinations and tests for preventive purposes. For example, some HMOs make regular eye examinations available to adults with diabetes, while others do not. Some HMOs make follow-up visits after hospitalization more available to their members than others. Women are particularly interested in screening examinations for breast and cervical cancers, a matter on which HMOs differ. Men are particularly interested in examinations for prostrate cancer, which is also a matter on which HMOs differ. HMOs also differ with regard to annual examinations, checkups for newborn babies and their mothers, visits to general physicians by well children, immunizations, and other matters.

It is important for you to know the circumstances under which each HMO will permit you to obtain care on an emergency basis. There are times, as a result of accidents or sudden illnesses, when medical care is needed immediately and there is no opportunity to make an appointment with your general physician and proceed in the customary manner. HMOs have special provisions for such needs, some of which require specific approval before any care may be obtained (*pre-approval*). Since these circumstances could arise at any time and could occur within the state where you live or outside of it, it is important that you understand what provisions different HMOs make for such possibilities.

Drug programs

The extraordinary cost of drugs and the frequent need for them today makes it essential that you familiarize yourself with the drug program offered by each HMO you are considering. Your concerns should be the completeness of the drug program you are considering and the terms of payment the HMO offers. Some HMO drug programs pay for nearly all of your likely drug costs, while others pay for little of such costs. Some HMO drug programs provide different payments for generic drugs and for brand-name drugs.

If you or a family member is utilizing a particular drug on an ongoing basis, an HMO's drug program will be very important to you. If you have been using a general physician, and particularly if you are planning to continue using him or her with your new HMO, the drug coverage possibilities of the different HMOs you are considering should be discussed with that physician. If you have been dealing with the same pharmacy for a number of years, and particularly if you know your pharmacist, that person can be useful in assessing drug programs.

<!-- checkmark -->
Dispute resolution
The matter of dispute resolution is important to you. This matter arises when a member of an HMO is not satisfied with the medical care the HMO is providing. Disputes can arise for many reasons. You may be dissatisfied with the care of a doctor or other provider. You may be dissatisfied with an HMO's decision not to provide a particular type of care, such as a referral to a specialist or a test or procedure. It is unlikely that you will agree with an HMO's decision regarding every medical matter and therefore, it is important to understand how disputes will be resolved when they arise.

<!-- checkmark -->
Physician preferences
Since there is general agreement between doctors and members regarding the quality of medical care of different HMOs, it is useful in making your comparison of HMOs to question as many doctors as possible. Be attentive to why doctors have elected to serve particular HMOs and not others. For example, it may be that an HMO's record of paying physicians for services has been poor. There are reported instances where bills of physicians have remained unpaid by an HMO for six months or longer.

Even if a physician elects to continue to serve an HMO with so poor a record of payment, it is possible that members of that HMO will not receive the most enthusiastic services from that physician. Bear in mind as you consider the opinions of physicians that every physician who works for HMOs has two interests to balance. On the one hand, he or she must provide his or her patients with the best possible medical care. On the other hand, he or she must cooperate with the HMO in its efforts to control costs.

Other sources of information

In addition to your broker, members of HMOs, and physicians involved with HMOs, there are other useful sources of information about the quality of care of HMOs. In some states, the state agency responsible for supervising HMOs prepares periodic reports evaluating HMOs in that state. Sometimes these evaluations are known as *HMO report cards*. Some of the factors frequently compared in these evaluations concern the different HMOs' procedures regarding particular medical care matters and the general opinions of members. Depending on how a state agency presents such reports, they may or may not be valuable to you. The most valuable report cards are those that present findings that clearly show the differences between the overall quality of care of different HMOs.

Various private sources also provide useful information about HMOs. One of these is some medical care companies that own HMOs. Obviously, anyone reading a comparison of HMOs by one of the competitors should take that fact into account in reviewing the information. Some medical care companies go out of their way to find materials that criticize their competitors, sometimes on grounds that are irrelevant to a realistic comparison. In reviewing these materials, you should consider precisely what points you are taking into account in comparing HMOs.

You will also find evaluations of HMOs in national magazines such as *U.S.News and World Report* and local magazines such as those that review activities in various cities. Some of these publications have been very precise about their recommendations. *U.S.News and World Report* provided readers with an *HMO Honor Roll,* naming twenty-one

HMOs that received its high four-star rating. In reviewing national publications, you must bear in mind that all the HMOs that are compared are not necessarily operating in your state.

Two other sources of information that may be useful are *Health Pages*, a consumer magazine that compares HMOs in different markets and *Families U.S.A. Foundation*, which publishes books about medical care including medical plans in various areas.

 History in your state

A matter of concern to you in selecting an HMO is how long different HMOs have been in business in your state and the best estimate of their staying power. Unfortunately, the entire medical care marketplace is in a state of change.

Providers of medical insurance make decisions to enter or leave particular states rapidly and sometimes with very little advance notice. These companies also frequently make decisions to change the programs they are offering in various ways.

There is no way to be certain that a particular HMO will be doing business in your state in future years. HMOs, like other medical care businesses, generally make only one-year commitments to members in their various contracts. Nevertheless, there are some indications of staying power that may assist you in making an estimate of whether an HMO is going to be doing business in your state in future years. Since a change in HMO is always difficult and time-consuming for members, and since a new HMO may not be dealing with the physicians you have relied on for medical care in the past, it is important to do your best to determine that the HMO you select will be there tomorrow. The track record of an HMO is the best indication of its likely conduct in the future.

HMOs that have stayed in particular states, particularly those that have stayed when markets for medical insurance have gone up and down, have demonstrated a reasonable commitment to continuing to do business in those states. HMOs that have substantial numbers of members in states are also more likely to remain. You can learn from the appropriate state office, a knowledgeable broker, and various available publications the number of members of different HMOs in your state. An HMO with a small membership may not have great incentive to stay in a particular state, while an HMO with a substantial membership (perhaps including large group policies with major employers) generally has such incentive.

Financial strength and affiliation

In addition to an HMO's history in your state and its membership size, you should be able to learn from your broker and other sources which HMOs you are considering are financially strong ones. The financial strength of HMOs is known to people in the industry and, from time to time, published in magazines.

Certain HMOs belong to large medical care insurance companies. This does not guarantee that an HMO's performance will be of high quality, but the reputation of such HMOs is usually well known and easy to learn. These HMOs are generally included in those discussed in state reports, national magazines, local magazines, and consumer reports.

Certain HMOs are associated with major university medical centers. These HMOs usually receive good evaluations. One of the things members seem to like about these HMOs is the availability of specialists, testing, and other necessary medical services from a large institution that they trust. Another benefit of these HMOs is that their general physicians are usually knowledgeable about the different medical services that are available in the medical centers and personally familiar with them. HMOs with this sort of association are not located in every geographic area. If, however, you live in an area where such an HMO exists, you should do everything possible to learn about it as you make your selection.

 ### National Committee for Quality Assurance ratings and accreditation

The *National Committee For Quality Assurance* (NCQA) is an accrediting body for HMOs. Since 1996, it has provided analysis reports concerning the quality of care of HMOs. This information is available by contacting:

NCQA Publications Center
P.O. Box 533
Annapolis Junction, MD 20701-0533
800-839-6487
www.ncqa.org

Although useful, this source of data is not the best basis of comparison of HMOs for several reasons. First, the analysis data, known as *Quality Compass*, is relatively new and still being formulated. Second, many HMOs have declined to participate in NCQA Quality Compass reviews for various reasons, including the belief of some HMOs that this way of analyzing their quality has not yet become sufficiently useful. Among the HMOs that have declined to participate are some that are considered to be of high quality. Therefore, it is not correct to conclude that HMOs not participating are simply those that know they will get a bad rating. Third, your particular needs and desires, and the available choices in your particular state may not make NCQA's analysis the most useful source of information for your personal situation. Although NCQA is a national accrediting organization that is receiving recognition, it does not provide each person seeking the best HMO with a one-stop way to make that determination.

The NCQA format of analysis is based on two broad categories—preventive measures and physicians. With regard to preventive measures, such as immunization, mammography, pap tests, and cholesterol tests, HMOs are rated by whether they do or do not make such preventive measures available. Accreditation and annual turnover are factors considered with regard to physicians. There are also factors based upon the percentage of board certified primary care physicians and specialists. While these factors should be considered, there are others of equal importance that do not appear in NCQA's rating system at the present time.

☑ Other national ratings

In addition to NCQA, some of the services that rate insurance companies generally have provided ratings for HMOs. For example, *A.M. Best Co.*, one of the major rating services with regard to insurance companies, has rated certain HMOs as having a *negative outlook*. According to A.M. Best Co., a negative outlook indicates that an HMO is experiencing unfavorable business trends that could result in a lowering of its rating if they continue. Since the company considers its *Superior* or *A+* rating to be important for HMOs, the negative outlook it has expressed is worth noting for those considering HMOs. However, it should not be taken out of the context of all the other factors. Information from national rating services is something your broker should be able to give you.

The best way to compare HMOs is to prepare a worksheet like the one shown on the following page. The factors to be considered are listed along the lefthand side of the chart, with the important ones at the top. The HMOs you are considering are listed across the top of the chart. The boxes at each intersection are completed by describing how each HMO is rated with regard to each factor. You can complete a chart like this very quickly with your independent broker, the input of a few friends, and perhaps a phone call to a physician you trust.

SAMPLE WORKSHEET FOR COMPARING HMOs

1 = Excellent   2 = Good   3 = Fair   4 = Poor

	HMO #1	HMO #2	HMO #3	HMO #4	HMO #5
QUALITY OF MEDICAL CARE PROVIDERS	___	___	___	___	___
COVERAGE FOR PRE-EXISTING ILLNESSES AND INJURIES	___	___	___	___	___
LEVEL OF SERVICE	___	___	___	___	___
COST	___	___	___	___	___
DRUG PROGRAMS	___	___	___	___	___
PHYSICIAN PREFERENCES	___	___	___	___	___
HISTORY IN YOUR STATE	___	___	___	___	___
PREVENTIVE AND EMERGENCY SERVICES	___	___	___	___	___
FINANCIAL STRENGTH AND AFFILIATION	___	___	___	___	___

- *This worksheet covers nine of the thirteen factors previously discussed, in order of importance to this person. Four factors, dispute resolution, other sources of information, National Committee for Quality Assurance Ratings and Accreditation, and other national ratings are less important to this person and, therefore, are not included. This person will probably choose HMO #2, since it gets the best overall rating after looking at this worksheet.*

• • • • •

Forming a Relationship with Your HMO

When you join an HMO, it is important to begin the relationship in the best possible manner. The quality of services you receive from your HMO will be enhanced if you follow a few simple principles in dealing with it.

Checklist for Forming a Relationship with Your HMO

- ❏ Familiarize yourself with your provider agreement and HMO's procedures
- ❏ Select your general physician
- ❏ Transfer all of your medical records to your general physician
- ❏ Learn the procedure for phone inquiries

☑ Familiarize yourself with your provider agreement and HMO's procedures

The first task for you (and any members of your family) is to understand your selected HMO's operating procedures. During your selection process, you should have reviewed the HMO's operating procedures to some extent, but once you are utilizing a particular HMO, you must review its procedures in detail. To use your HMO effectively, you and each covered member of your family must know what the HMO requires for you to receive medical treatment, how your general physician is used, what drug coverage is provided, what to do in emergencies, how to get care from specialists, how to obtain tests, and what preventive services including annual examinations are covered. You should also become familiar with the forms of treatment that are *not* covered by your HMO, as well as the forms of treatment for which coverage is limited. The first step in familiarizing yourself with these matters is to read your HMO contract (your *provider agreement*) carefully.

☑ Select your general physician

Once you understand the basic operating structure of your HMO, you should begin your relationship with your general physician. If you have selected your HMO because the general physician you (and possibly your family members) have been utilizing is on its approved list, this will be much simpler. If not, you should carefully select your general physician from the HMO's approved list. Ask questions of others whose opinions you respect and meet or at least speak with each of the general physicians you are considering.

☑ Transfer all of your medical records to your general physician

An essential part of the introductory process is for you to arrange to send all medical records for you (and your family) to your new general physician. Remember that some medical records, such as x-rays, CAT scans, MRIs, sonograms, and some medical reports are often retained at hospitals or other facilities you may have visited. Discuss with your new general physician whether to obtain copies of these records for him or her or simply advise him or her of the location of such records should they ever be needed. If you are taking any medications or undergoing any form of ongoing medical care at the time you begin a relationship with your new general physician, those matters should be reviewed with him or her immediately.

☑ Learn the procedure for phone inquiries

A good deal of medical care takes place without the patient actually going to see the physician. Everyone makes phone calls to physicians to ask whether something should be done about a condition that is not particularly severe or whether a condition requires an appointment with the physician. Different physicians serving HMOs handle these situations in different ways. One of the first things you should do when you establish a relationship with your new general physician is determine how that physician handles telephone inquiries and whether there is someone in the physician's office to whom such inquiries should be addressed when the physician is unavailable.

If you are in doubt whether your new general physician wants you to proceed in a particular manner, ask the physician. If you feel that something is occurring between you and your general physician that is not consistent with your best medical care, tell the physician. Although some physicians are not flexible in the way they deal with patients, many physicians are willing to vary their approach within limitations placed upon them by the HMO.

• • • • •

Specialists, Testing, Drugs, and Other Medical Care

General or primary care physicians for HMOs are provided with direct and indirect incentives to limit the use of specialists, testing, drugs, and other types of medical care. This has proven to be a controversial and difficult matter. As an individual member of an HMO, you are not going to change this fact of medical care life. Your concern is obtaining the best possible medical care for you and members of your family. There are useful steps you may take in that regard.

Checklist for Obtaining Specialists, Testing, Drugs, and Other Medical Care

- ❏ Read the requirements in your provider agreement
- ❏ Ask your general physician to consider the request
- ❏ Ask your general physician specific questions about tests and referrals
- ❏ Advise your general physician of continuing symptoms
- ❏ Advise your general physician of opinions of others
- ❏ Ask your general physician if he or she has told you of all possibilities for treating your condition
- ❏ Ask your general physician about obtaining a second opinion
- ❏ Tell your general physician that you are planning to discuss the matter with others

☑ Read the requirements in your provider agreement

You must comply carefully with all the requirements of your HMO. Failing to comply with requirements of your HMO, including keeping appointments and paying your portion of its bills on time, provides the HMO with an excuse for failing to respond to your medical needs as fully and promptly as you would like. You will find the requirements of your HMO in the materials it provides to you when you enroll. Read those requirements carefully and remember the importance of complying with them.

☑ Ask your general physician to consider the request

Your first line of attack for getting specialized or other medical care from someone other than your general physician is your general physician. In functioning as the gatekeeper, your general physician determines whether to refer you for specialized or other medical care. Even though economic pressures exist, general physicians for HMOs are often reluctant to reject other medical care when doing so would clearly be against the best medical interests of a patient. However, since such decisions are often in the gray range, it is up to you to discuss the matter of care beyond that of your general physician with him or her and be certain that he or she takes a clear position on whether to refer you for other medical care.

Although your and your family's concern is receiving the best possible medical care and not the compensation of HMO physicians, you will receive the best services from HMO physicians if you are sensitive to the fact that their compensation is strictly controlled. Reasonable and ethical physicians recognize that the manner in which their fees are paid today is less than ideal for both parties. The relationship between HMO members and HMO physicians works best when both parties recognize that they are working in a system neither of them designed.

Ask your general physician specific questions about tests and referrals

You will sometimes find that asking the right questions of your general physician accomplishes your purpose. You might ask, for example, *Do you think I should have a blood test to try to learn more about what is going on?* or *Do you think that my condition has reached the point where I should be seeing a urologist?* Since one thought on every general physician's mind is possible malpractice, physicians who might otherwise remain silent are sometimes reluctant to go on record as giving negative answers to such questions. They are aware that their patient's condition may become worse and, sooner or later, someone may realize that the patient should have been referred for testing, a specialty consultation, or something else.

☑ Advise your general physician of continuing symptoms

When you believe that care beyond your general physician is required, but your general physician will not refer you for such care, it is time to turn up the gas a little. One way to do this is to make a phone call to your general physician and explain that your symptoms continue to persist and you are becoming anxious about them. Specifically request your general physician to inform you what further steps he or she has decided to take and what advice he or she can provide. It is very important that this conversation with your general physician makes it absolutely clear that it is your understanding that your general physician has decided not to refer you for additional care and that you are concerned about that decision. If you let the conversation end with a *wait-and-see* decision, you will be letting your general physician off the hook and not encouraging him or her to refer you for the additional care.

☑ Advise your general physician of opinions of others

Another way to keep such a matter on your general physician's mind is to suggest that the possibility of another doctor has come into the picture. You should not do this in a hostile way, but simply as part of letting your general physician know what is concerning you. Remarks such as, *My sister is very concerned about my condition and she mentioned it to her doctor who said it really sounded as though I should be seeing a gastroenterologist,* or *A friend of mine had the same symptoms I am having a few years ago, and she was referred to a cardiologist who did a couple of tests and prescribed something for the pain* are quite natural and relatively innocent, but they let your general physician know you are receiving information about what other doctors might say about your condition. Since general physicians used by HMOs have some discretion even under the worst circumstances, this approach may prove to be sufficient to get you the specialty care or testing you want to receive.

 Ask your general physician if he or she has told you of all possibilities for treating your condition

Some HMOs encourage their general physicians to follow what is known as the *gag rule*. The gag rule, an extremely controversial matter regarding HMOs, prevents a physician from telling you about the availability of certain possibilities for the treatment of your condition. As a result, there may be instances when members of an HMO do not receive full information about their treatment options. When this occurs, it is impossible for you to make a good decision about how to proceed with your medical care.

If you suspect that your general physician has not told you about every reasonable possibility for your treatment, you should do several things immediately. The first thing to do is schedule a face-to-face appointment with your general physician. At that meeting, ask him or her point-blank questions like the following.

- What are *all* the medical possibilities available to me for this condition?
- Have we discussed *every* reasonable option I have for dealing with my condition?
- Is there any other information I might obtain from testing or anything else that would help me make the best possible decision?

Although you do not know exactly what your HMO requires of your general physician regarding providing information to you, this sort of direct question makes it very difficult for most physicians to withhold important information.

☑ **Ask your general physician about obtaining a second opinion**

The next thing you should do is tell your general physician that since the matter is so serious, you would like a second opinion. Your HMO contract may entitle you to such an opinion and, if not, there is nothing to prevent you from obtaining it at your own expense. Your second opinion request lets your general physician know that his or her advice will soon be going head-to-head with the advice of another physician. If you continue to believe that important information is being withheld from you, you should definitely consult another physician even if it means spending some of your own money.

☑ **Tell your general physician that you are planning to discuss the matter with others**

The next thing you should do in this situation is let your general physician know you are planning to discuss the matter with other people such as family members or friends. This will suggest to most general physicians that there is a reasonable chance that you will be pursuing the matter further. General physicians want to keep HMOs happy, but they do not want to be found negligent doing so.

• • • • •

Resolving Disputes

Although the techniques previously mentioned for further testing work a good deal of the time, there are situations when a member of an HMO cannot obtain the treatment he or she feels is necessary no matter what informal steps are taken. When that occurs, you will need to resort to formal steps to provide you with the best chance for obtaining the care you need.

Even if you have selected your HMO carefully and done everything correctly to establish a good relationship with it, you may sometimes have disputes. Disputes will always boil down to one thing—money. Sometimes you may want a second opinion or a particular treatment that your HMO does not want to provide. You may want drugs or other items that your HMO contends are unnecessary.

Unless what you are seeking is clearly excluded from coverage in your Provider Agreement, in which case you are simply out of luck, the matter is always debatable. The first line of attack is an appeal to your general physician. General physicians are often caught between a rock and a hard place on such matters, but with a little diplomacy they may come around to your position. After that, there is a review procedure set forth in your Provider Agreement. Usually the review involves at least one appeal to a reviewing authority within the HMO and, thereafter, a reviewing authority in your state government.

Disputes with an HMO arise when you are unable to obtain the medical care you need by informal means. Unless there is a provision in your HMO contract excluding the particular medical care from coverage, the issue between you and the HMO may take several forms. Sometimes an HMO contends that the medical care you are seeking is unnecessary. At other times, HMOs contend that another form of medical care (invariably less expensive) is sufficient. HMOs also claim at times that the medical care you are seeking for your particular condition is not recommended or is experimental. When your HMO's reason for denying you the medical care you are seeking depends upon medical judgment, your HMO will have at its disposal physicians that will assist it.

Checklist for Resolving Disputes with Your HMO

- ❏ Discuss the matter thoroughly with your primary care physician
- ❏ Discuss the matter thoroughly with the appropriate HMO representative
- ❏ Write a certified mail, return receipt requested letter to the appropriate person at the HMO
- ❏ Utilize the review procedure set forth in your provider agreement
- ❏ Request a review by an appropriate state agency
- ❏ Consider the appropriateness of an arbitration action or a lawsuit

 Discuss the matter thoroughly with your primary care physician

When it comes to rendering you the best possible medical care without running afoul of the wishes of an HMO, your general physician is somewhat between a rock and a hard place. On the one hand, he or she does not want to lose the ability to work for the HMO and to serve patients like you. On the other hand, he or she wants to render the best medical care possible to his or her patients. In most instances, when push comes to shove, a conscientious physician will go to the wall to try to do what is proper for a patient. Give your general physician the chance to do this, but, if it fails, go on to the next step.

 Discuss the matter thoroughly with the appropriate HMO representative

Every HMO has some sort of review hierarchy. Sometimes it is another physician, sometimes it is a medical administrator, and sometimes it is both. In many instances, these individuals behave more or less like robots. The question before them is whether the patient is really entitled to the medical care he or she is requesting and whether the HMO is likely to run into difficulty if it does not provide it. These discussions between a patient and the reviewing authority at the HMO tend to be most effective when it is clear that the patient is fully aware of his or her rights.

A reference in your conversation to the appropriate section of your provider agreement or the suggestion that you have spoken with someone outside the HMO who is knowledgeable about your medical difficulty are usually useful. However, these discussions often center around whether another form of medical care would be sufficient for your condition.

HMOs also argue at times that the medical care you are seeking is not recommended or is experimental. If you can obtain an outside medical opinion that you need the medical treatment you are seeking, that is usually very helpful.

Write a certified mail, return receipt requested letter to the appropriate person at the HMO

A letter from you sent in this fashion is a wake-up call when an HMO receives it. It knows because you have taken the time and spent the money to have the letter certified that you are taking the matter very seriously. It also knows, since someone in the HMO must sign the receipt, that you have acquired proof that you have given the HMO the information in the letter.

In your letter, summarize your condition and be very specific about the dates you have seen your general physician, the tests you have undergone, the course of action your general physician has prescribed, and all other relevant matters. If you have consulted an outside physician, mention that physician. If your HMO has not provided you with a reason for denying the medical treatment you are seeking, request that it do so. Letters like this should be typed, carefully written, and stick to the point. Try not to criticize your general physician any more than necessary. Even though your general physician works for the HMO, he or she may be on your side in the matter and, if so, you want to keep him or her there.

The purpose of writing letters to HMOs when there are disputes is to get their business interests working for you. An HMO's business interests are making as much money as possible and providing as little medical care as possible, without getting in trouble with state authorities and without being forced to defend expensive lawsuits. Letters from a member that confirm particular matters are unpleasant for HMOs, since those letters make a record for future purposes that HMOs would prefer did not exist. Such letters take the wiggle room out of the HMO. It cannot say that you did not specifically request particular medical care when a letter from you clearly confirms that you did request it. It cannot say that it was unaware that you received a medical opinion that supports your request when you have written confirmation that you told that to the HMO. Explanations such as, *We thought we had agreed on a wait-and-see approach to her condition* or *She did not explain her entire history when we made our determination* simply do not fly when properly written letters confirm that the situation was otherwise.

If the person reviewing letters like this at your HMO feels you are making a good case for your state agency or a court some day, the HMO will think twice about continuing to deny the requested medical care. If such letters find their way to lawyers for the HMO, the lawyers will decide whether the HMO is likely to suffer harm before the state agency or a court. If the lawyers feel that the HMO is threatened by its current position, they will advise the HMO to change it. Properly prepared letters are a very valuable tool for getting HMOs to provide medical care they do not want to provide. The best letters are those your HMO would not like to be read to state agencies or courts because they show that it did not provide medical care that was reasonable and necessary under the circumstances.

Bearing these thoughts in mind, there are four points that are particularly important to make in letters to your HMO.

1. *A review of the history of your condition, the medical steps that have been taken, and their results to date.* Your review should be as specific as possible, including dates. The last item in this review should be your request for the medical services that are being denied by your HMO. Write this review in a manner that makes clear how your situation has progressed and why it is necessary that the services you are requesting be provided. Be sure to include in this point a statement that your health is being permanently injured by your HMO's refusal to provide you with further medical care.

2. *The opinion of a physician that you require the medical services you are being denied.* It may be necessary for you to spend your own money to obtain the support of an outside physician for this purpose, but if your condition is serious, you have no other choice. If possible, a letter of opinion from the outside physician should be included. There is nothing more influential than such a letter in these circumstances, especially if the physician's reasons for his or her opinion are carefully explained.

3. *A request that your HMO provide to you in writing its specific reasons for not providing you with the requested medical services.* Include a request that the names of the physicians whose opinions are being relied upon by the HMO be disclosed to you. Although this will frequently not occur, it is important to make such a request since your HMO may realize when you do that

it is unable to support its position with medical authority. Physicians employed by HMOs, and indeed all physicians, provide verbal opinions far more easily than written ones.

4. *Advise your HMO that if the medical care you are requesting is not provided, legal action will be taken.*

A sample letter is provided.

Sample Letter to HMO that Refuses to Provide a Specialist

```
217 Washington Boulevard
Tucson, Arizona 00000

October 23, 2005
CERTIFIED MAIL
RETURN RECEIPT REQUESTED

Ms. Beatrice R. Sweeney
Member Relations Manager
Pridecare Health Management Organization
16 Nevada Street
Tucson, Arizona 00000

Re: Member No. 000-00-0000

Dear Ms. Sweeney:
I am writing to demand that you immediately refer me to a gastrointestinal specialist for the extreme stomach pain I have been experiencing for several months. The history of this matter is as follows: On September 19, 2005, I had an appointment with Dr. Irene B. Cooleridge, my primary care physician. I told Dr. Cooleridge about the pain I was experiencing and she examined me. At the end of my visit, Dr. Cooleridge recommended that I use Maalox for the next eight weeks and eat a bland diet. I immediately began doing those things.
```

After two weeks had passed, my symptoms not only failed to improve, but they got worse. I telephoned Dr. Cooleridge and requested that she see me immediately. It was three days before Dr. Cooleridge was able to see me, and once she did, she told me to keep on doing the same thing.

A week later I was in so much pain that I was unable to attend work. I telephoned Dr. Cooleridge and asked for an appointment on an emergency basis. When I went to Dr. Cooleridge's office, which was on October 13, I requested that she immediately refer me to a gastrointestinal specialist. Dr. Cooleridge indicated that she would discuss the matter with my HMO and advise me promptly. The next day I received a telephone call from Dr. Cooleridge's secretary saying that I had not been approved for referral to a specialist. I went to the emergency room of Baycrest General Hospital the next day and was told by Dr. Brian Westerly that I needed to see a gastrointestinal specialist immediately.

My provider agreement with your HMO indicates that I will receive a specialty referral when that is reasonably necessary. Such a referral is not only reasonably necessary in this instance, it is essential. If for any reason you do not intend to provide this referral, please advise me in writing of your reasons and the names of the physicians whose opinions you are relying upon. I can no longer endure the pain my stomach distress is causing me.

If you do not immediately provide for my referral to a gastrointestinal specialist, I will follow the review procedure set out in my provider agreement. That procedure entitles me to bring the matter to the attention of the state health regulatory agency for its review of your denial. I hope that this will not be necessary, but I must receive appropriate medical care for my condition.

Sincerely,
Jessica Winterstein

☑ Utilize the review procedure set forth in your provider agreement

The next step in the process of seeking to change a decision of your HMO to deny medical care is for you to utilize the grievance procedure set forth in your provider agreement. It is important that you pursue your grievance precisely in accordance with the terms of your contract, including timing and other specific requirements. If you fail to do this, your HMO will assert that you are not entitled to the medical services you are seeking because you did not comply with the terms of your contract. If you have any doubt about what is required in order to comply with your contract, get help immediately from someone who is competent to advise you of what you need to do.

The review procedure established by most HMOs consists of an in-house review first followed by a review by a designated state agency. Assuming that you have already spoken with a representative at your HMO and written the certified mail, return receipt requested letter discussed, the only thing you need to do regarding the in-house review is make sure that you have complied precisely with the requirements of your provider agreement. This may consist simply of designating the materials you have already supplied as a formal appeal. If you have any doubt that you have followed the review procedure correctly, check with the HMO and confirm what you are doing in a further letter to it.

You may want to consider obtaining the assistance of a lawyer at this point, depending upon the seriousness of the particular matter. If you do choose to do this, prepare a very complete chronology of all of your dealings in the matter so far. This will enable the lawyer to understand the full scope of the matter very quickly and will save you money in legal fees. You may also find in some instances that the insurance broker who provided you with coverage, or the insurance broker for your employer if that is how you obtained coverage, may be of assistance to you. Some brokers are quite adept at convincing medical insurers of all types to authorize particular services. This is particularly true when the broker has a good deal of business with the insurer, such as with an HMO.

☑ Request a review by an appropriate state agency

At this point, a lawyer who has dealt with such matters can be very useful. Every state agency has its own quirks and the people in it their own personalities. If you take the step of going to your state agency, be sure of two things. First, be sure that the matter is significant enough to justify the effort. Save your ammunition for the important fights, since there is no point in knocking yourself out over a small medical expense or difference of opinion of little consequence. Second, be sure that you have provided your lawyer with a very complete chronology of relevant events and all of your medical records. The review procedure of your state agency should be followed carefully and you should be fully prepared to present your best case.

☑ Consider the appropriateness of an arbitration action or a lawsuit

Many provider agreements provide for *arbitration* if all else fails. In fact, quite a few states require HMO contracts to contain a provision advising members that disputes will be resolved by arbitration. If you reach the point where you are seriously considering arbitration or a lawsuit, it is definitely time to engage a lawyer. These procedures are fairly long and difficult and, unfortunately, costly. A very small percentage of disputes with HMOs go this far and, hopefully, you will never experience one of them.

CHAPTER 9

Life and Disability Insurance

The first thing to say about life insurance is that if you do not have responsibilities for others, you do not need it. Insurance agents will tell you that life insurance is necessary to protect your estate. If you are not responsible for anyone else, you can take the risk of dying and do not need to protect your estate for anyone. If you do decide to buy life insurance, be sure you understand what kind of life insurance you are buying.

> ### Terms Used in Life Insurance Policies
>
> **beneficiary.** The person who will receive money under a life insurance policy.
>
> **benefit.** The amount a life insurance policy will pay upon the insured's death (some life insurance policies also pay a benefit if the insured loses an arm, leg, or eye).
>
> **borrowing capacity.** The amount of money that may be borrowed under a whole life insurance policy at various times.
>
> **cash surrender value.** The amount of money an insured may receive for turning in a whole life insurance policy at various times.

double indemnity. Payment of twice the face value of a life insurance policy (some life insurance policies pay double indemnity for accidental death).

guaranteed renewable term insurance. A term life insurance policy that is guaranteed to be renewable for a certain number of years.

insured person. The person whose life is insured under a life insurance policy.

owner. The person who owns a life insurance policy.

preexisting condition exclusion. An illness or injury someone has before the term of a life insurance policy and which cannot be used as a basis for receiving a benefit.

premium. The annual cost of a life insurance policy.

rating of insurance company. The quality of an insurance company determined by the rating agencies.

term life insurance. A life insurance policy that is in force for only the term during which premium payments are made.

whole life insurance. A life insurance policy in which the insurance continues after the last payment is made and there is a cash surrender value and borrowing capacity.

Checklist for Purchasing Life Insurance

❑ Determine the risks you want to protect against, how much money will be needed to protect against them, and how long they will last

❑ Decide whether term life insurance or whole life insurance will best meet your needs

❑ Select an independent broker who sells life insurance policies from numerous companies and has no special relationship to any of them

❑ Request the broker to provide you with at least three choices of companies and compare their life insurance policies

❑ Verify that the companies you are considering are highly rated

❑ Review the life insurance policy you select and ask your broker any questions you have about it

❑ Review your choice of beneficiaries with your accountant or tax preparer

❑ Obtain a copy of your life insurance policy (not simply a summary of it) and place it in an identified folder in your record box

❑ Advise one or more people who will be aware of your death of the existence of your life insurance policy

☑ Determine the risks you want to protect against, how much money will be needed to protect against them, and how long they will last

If it is necessary for you to buy life insurance, or if you simply want to do so, the first issue for you to address is the risk you want to protect against. For example, if you are a single parent with a four-year-old child and you want to be sure that if you die you leave enough money to care for your child and provide for a college education, you need a certain amount of life insurance for the next eighteen years. If you have no dependents but have a brother you would like to leave some money if you die, you must think carefully about the amount of money you want to leave your brother and how much it is worth to you to be able to do so. Once you have decided what it is you wish to protect, you can figure out the amount of money necessary for that protection with reasonable accuracy. Do not forget to take into account everything other than life insurance you will leave when you die. This process is known *as estate planning* and you must think about it if you are seriously considering life insurance. Also, if you are thinking about life insurance, it is probably time for you to think about your first will. (This is discussed in Chapter 2.)

There are some tax issues and other things to take into account as to either term or whole life insurance. You may want to talk to a lawyer or accountant about them. Do not rush into life insurance because someone tells you that everyone needs to have it. If life insurance comes with your job at an inexpensive cost or no cost to you, you may feel it makes sense to take it. If, however, you have to pay the premiums yourself, life insurance may not be a high-priority item for you until other people depend upon you for their living expenses.

 Decide whether term life insurance or whole life insurance will best meet your needs

There are many different forms of life insurance, which insurance salespeople like to refer to as *products*. You could spend your life trying to understand all of the differences between different life insurance policies. Unless your financial life becomes very complicated, what you need to know is simply the difference between *term* life insurance and *whole* life insurance.

Term Life Insurance. *Term life insurance* is life insurance that you may continue to purchase for a defined term. Generally the term is fairly long. Ten-year and twenty-year terms are typical. With term life insurance, you receive nothing other than the insurance during each year for which you pay. You pay a *premium* for the insurance each year and when the year is over, you have nothing unless you buy the next year's term insurance.

When you buy term life insurance, you must be certain that it is *guaranteed renewable*. This means that you are entitled by your insurance agreement to purchase the insurance for the agreed number of years. You must also be certain that the term life insurance is guaranteed to be renewable for a stated premium. Guaranteed renewable insurance is worthless unless the premium is guaranteed. Often the agreed premium changes after a certain number of years and this may occur more than once. If you buy twenty-year guaranteed renewable term life insurance, the premiums for all twenty years must be acceptable to you.

Term life insurance is most useful when you have a good plan for your retirement and possible disability, but there are particular needs that could not be handled if you died somewhere along the line. Generally, needs like this have to do with children, but that is not always the case. For example, if you are paying off a significant business expense that will be on your back for the next ten years, the possibility of purchasing term life insurance to cover that risk for the ten-year period might be sensible. In these types of situations, term life insurance can be very useful.

Whole Life Insurance. As distinguished from term life insurance, *whole life insurance* is a growing financial asset that you own, as you are paying for it and someday have paid off. When you buy whole life insurance, you get a number of things you do not get with term life insurance. First, once the agreed amount of time when premiums must be paid has passed, the life insurance policy remains in force. For example, if you bought a whole life insurance policy that was paid up after twenty years (at an agreed premium each year you would continue to have the life insurance for the rest of your life.

Whole life insurance also has what is known as a *cash surrender value*. A cash surrender value is a value that you could get by turning in your life insurance policy in the future. The cash surrender value gets larger as you make more premium payments over the years. In addition, many whole life insurance policies have a provision for borrowing certain amounts of money as the policy is paid off. Like cash surrender values, the amounts you may borrow grow as the years pass.

Whole life insurance is preferred by people who sell insurance because it is more expensive and, therefore, the commissions the insurance companies pay them are larger. If you want to leave to someone else insurance that will continue to have value after you have paid it off, whole life insurance is probably the right choice.

 Select an independent broker who sells life insurance policies from numerous companies and has no special relationship to any of them

An independent broker is one who does not work for any single life insurance company. He or she represents a range of companies and can make recommendations based on the comparison of the policies from different companies. Independent insurance brokers generally identify themselves in several ways. Some belong to associations that require their members to be independent. You can learn from any broker whether he or she belongs to such an association. In addition, brokers that sell insurance from a number of unrelated companies are generally independent, since a broker who works for or has an association with only one insurance company does not do so. The best way to determine whether a broker is independent is to ask him or her whether he or she is independent and what companies' insurance policies he or she is able to sell to you.

 Request the broker to provide you with at least three choices of companies and compare their life insurance policies

Pricing quotations from three good companies should give you a reliable idea of what is sensible to pay for any form of insurance. If one of the prices is much higher or much lower than the other two, go with one of the other companies.

 Verify that the companies you are considering are highly rated

Life insurance companies are rated in a number of places. The most well-known sources are *Moody's*, *A.M. Best's*, and *Standard and Poor*. Anyone who sells life insurance can explain the rating system to you, which is not difficult to understand. All three of these ratings services use A, B, and C categories for ratings purposes. In addition, each of these rating services has various sub-categories, such as AA or AAA, which indicate the position of a company within the A, B, or C category. The rating services also distinguish between long-term credit and short-term credit.

Since the entire A category is limited to companies that have excellent and clearly superior credit ratings, the safest course of action for you is to limit your choices to A-rated companies. As with any form of insurance, the rating of the companies you are considering is one of the important factors you should take into account.

Review the life insurance policy you select and ask your broker any questions you have about it

Reading an insurance policy is pretty boring and sometimes the language of it is difficult to understand. One of the reasons for using an independent broker is so that person will be available to explain provisions of the policy that are unclear. It is a good idea to read the policy you are buying carefully and mark each of the places that you do not fully understand. Then ask your independent broker your questions all at one time. Another good person to ask about the provisions of the life insurance policy is an accountant.

Do not get hung up on too much of the legalese. The most important things you want to know are how much the policy pays if you die, how much the policy costs you each year, and how long the policy is guaranteed renewable at a predetermined price.

 Review your choice of beneficiaries with your accountant or tax preparer

You should obviously do this any time you purchase any form of insurance. Most life insurance policies require you to select a primary beneficiary and a secondary beneficiary. The secondary beneficiary will receive the payment if the primary beneficiary is no longer living. If you are using a lawyer to prepare a will for you, this matter should be reviewed with that lawyer.

 Obtain a copy of your life insurance policy (not simply a summary of it) and place it in an identified folder in your record box

Obtain and retain an exact, complete copy of any insurance policy you purchase. Some insurance companies send insured persons addenda to insurance policies from time-to-time. Keep any of these with your insurance policy. Do not wait until you have a claim or someone else makes one against you before you try to find your insurance policy.

 Advise one or more people who will be aware of your death of the existence of your life insurance policy

Your accountant or tax preparer, if you use one regularly, would be a good person for this purpose. If you are dealing with a lawyer you intend to have continuing relations with, he or she is also a good choice. If you live with a spouse or other partner, you may want to keep your insurance policies in a place such as a safe deposit box that is accessible by either of you.

• • • • •

Disability Insurance

Disability, like illness or injury, is a very serious problem for anyone. It is particularly serious for people who need to earn money to support themselves and perhaps others. Unfortunately, the possibility of disability is difficult to deal with.

If you are one of the fortunate people who works for an employer that offers participation in a disability plan and if your part of the cost is bearable for you, go for it. If your employer offers a choice of long-term and short-term disability plans and the cost of both is too great for you to bear, choose the long-term disability plan if you can afford it. A short-term disability, of perhaps three or six months, is terrible but it may be financially bearable. A long-term disability, which may mean disability for an entire lifetime, is never financially bearable. Follow the rule that you buy insurance for risks you cannot afford to take.

Before discussing what to look for if you buy disability insurance, it is worth spending a little time discussing the possible ways to financially deal with disability.

Checklist of Possible Sources of Money in the Event of Disability

- ❏ Savings and investments
- ❏ Social Security and Medicare
- ❏ Third-party awards
- ❏ Earnings from alternative employment
- ❏ Disability insurance payments

☑ Savings and investments

The use of savings and investments is obvious, but very few people have much of them early in their careers. If you do have some savings or investments, your aim if you become disabled is to use them to provide the most monthly income to you without risking the funds that you have. Many retirement plans have a provision permitting them to be utilized in the event of disability. If you have a plan and there is a significant amount of money in it, you should consider this as part of your savings and investments.

☑ Social Security and Medicare

Eligibility for Social Security and Medicare at the time of disability is a very technical matter. It depends in part on your condition, in part on how much you have paid into the Social Security trust fund, and in part on some other matters. Hopefully this is something your accountant will be able to help you deal with if that becomes necessary. If not, there are people including some lawyers who specialize in getting people enrolled in these programs.

You should be aware of two possible problems if you pursue Social Security or Medicare for a disability. One problem is that you do not want to pay any more than you have to for assistance in getting enrolled. Check this matter out with your accountant and people who have faced the same circumstances. The second problem is that there are serious limitations on what you can earn from work while you are receiving these benefits.

Go over this matter carefully with your accountant or the person you are relying on for Social Security and Medicare advice. Even if these benefits are available to you, it may not be worth taking them when all the financial consequences are considered. A personal statement of your disability benefits is available from the Social Security Administration at their website (**www.ssa.gov**) or by sending in form SSA-7004, which is available at your local Social Security Office.

✓ Third-party awards

Possible monies from third parties fall into two groups. The first includes workers' compensation you may be entitled to if you are injured or become ill as a result of your job and unemployment insurance you may be entitled to when you cannot work. These benefits are determined by state law. If you work for a company, there should be someone available to advise you how to apply for these benefits. Employers are required by state law to cover their employees in these ways, and someone in your company should be able to help you prepare the paperwork and take the necessary steps to receive these monies. You can also call the state agencies that are responsible for these matters and there will be someone who is able to tell you what you should do.

The other type of third-party benefit is a damage award from someone who is responsible for your disability. A simple case would be when someone was negligent and injured you in a car or other type of accident. This is a matter where you would need to use a lawyer. There are a lot of sources of information about lawyers, but the best source is their former clients. Ask your friends and relatives what lawyers they have used for different types of matters. Speak with a few of those lawyers and choose the one who is most comfortable and confidence-inspiring for you.

☑ Earnings from alternative employment

Alternative employment often presents a whole range of possibilities. If you are engaged in physical labor, disability for you may come about as a result of bad knees or too much neck pain. You may not be able to do your physical work any longer, but you might be an ideal estimator or inspector or be able to do some other job that uses all your knowledge and experience. If you used to travel for your job, but are no longer able to travel, you may be able to do a home-based business using your old skills for something new. It does not hurt to think about these possibilities and explore them a little, even if you are in perfect health and have no concern about that changing.

☑ Disability insurance payments

For most people, the monthly income they will receive from the other four sources will not provide them with the lifestyle they would like to have if they became disabled. If your disability is not due to something that gives you a claim against someone and if you are planning to pursue some type of alternative employment that is inconsistent with Social Security and Medicare benefits, then the sources of money for you is narrowed considerably. Since this is often the case, disability insurance becomes something that may be worth considering.

Terms Used in Disability Insurance Policies

benefit period. The length of time that one receives disability payments under a disability insurance policy.

guaranteed renewable disability policy. A disability insurance policy that is guaranteed renewable for a certain number of years.

monthly benefit amount. The amount of money paid each month to a person who is totally or partially disabled.

own occupation disability insurance. Disability insurance that pays you if you are unable to do your own occupation, even though you may be able to do others.

partial disability. Inability to do some of your work, but not all of it.

period of contestability. The time within which the insurance company may challenge the validity of a disability insurance policy.

permanent illness or injury. An illness or injury that will last for as long as a person lives.

preexisting condition exclusion. A provision in a disability insurance policy that prevents you from obtaining payments if an illness or injury existed before the term of the policy began.

premium. The cost per year of a disability insurance policy.

rating of insurance company. The quality of an insurance company determined by the rating agencies.

temporary illness or injury. An illness or injury that should go away in a reasonable amount of time, usually ninety days or six months.

> **term.** The length of time for which a disability insurance policy can remain in effect.
> **total disability.** Inability to do one's work to a reasonable extent.
> **waiver of premium provision.** A provision in a disability insurance policy that excuses a person from further payments because of disability.

• • • • •

How to Obtain Disability Insurance

Disability insurance that is provided and paid for in part by your employer is a no-brainer. The chance that you will be able to get better disability insurance at a cost you can afford is small to zero. Unless there is something clearly wrong with the disability insurance an employer is offering, an employee who wants to have disability insurance should consider it very seriously.

When there is no such possibility, which is the case with many employers, or when you are self-employed, there are specific things to look for to select the best disability insurance coverage on your own.

Checklist for Obtaining a Disability Insurance Policy

- ❑ Determine if you belong to any association that offers you disability insurance
- ❑ Select a competent independent insurance broker
- ❑ Obtain at least three proposals from highly rated insurance companies
- ❑ Select insurance coverage that is as close as possible to *own occupation*
- ❑ Obtain sufficient coverage to meet your needs
- ❑ Choose a reasonable exclusionary period
- ❑ Choose the duration for which benefits will be paid
- ❑ Be sure that there is coverage for *partial disability*
- ❑ Be sure your policy contains a *waiver of premium* provision
- ❑ Be sure the premium is guaranteed for a reasonably long period of time
- ❑ Be sure that the *period of contestability* is two years or less
- ❑ Obtain a full copy of your disability insurance policy

☑ Determine if you belong to any association that offers you disability insurance

The first thing to do if you are looking for disability insurance is check the offerings of every association of which you are a member. If you are in a union, check with the union. If you are in any form of occupation-related group, check with it. Check with your credit union if you belong to one. Group offerings of disability insurance are often more affordable and may have better terms than policies you could go out and buy yourself.

☑ Select a competent independent insurance broker

If disability insurance coverage is not available to you through an association, your next move is to find a good independent broker. It is important to understand something about brokers in order to do this. Three kinds of people sell insurance. People who are employed by an insurance company to sell its policies. Forget about these people, as their interest is to sell their company's product. The second kind of person is known as an *agent*. Agents sometimes serve one company and sometimes several companies. Although some agents try to be fairer with their customers than others, you should avoid agents for the same reason as avoiding a person employed by an insurance company. What you want is an independent broker, whose only interest is in selling you insurance from the insurance company that is best for you. There are associations of independent brokers such as the *National Association of Health Underwriters* and various similar local associations. Do not be shy about asking brokers you are considering if they belong to such associations and what assurance you have that they are independent.

A good broker is someone who is very familiar with the insurance policies offered in a particular field and willing to spend time with customers to answer their questions and assure them of making the best possible selection. Disability insurance is long-lasting and serves a critical purpose. If you can find a broker who has a lot of knowledge and time to spend with you on both disability and medical insurance, you have definitely found someone worth using. You do not need to be concerned about the broker's fees since they are paid by the insurance company. Your best guide for selecting an independent broker is the advice of people you know who are using that person.

Obtain at least three proposals from highly rated insurance companies

Like with life insurance policies, getting proposals from at least three good companies should give you a reliable idea of what is sensible for you to pay.

 Select insurance coverage that is as close as possible to own occupation

The best type of disability insurance is *own occupation*. This form of disability insurance makes payments to you if you are unable to do your present work, regardless of your ability to do something else. Unfortunately, this form of disability insurance is vanishing and being replaced by disability insurance that has two kinds of limitations. One kind of limitation defines your occupation more generally than what you are specifically doing at present. For example, if you are a salesperson or customer service representative and you make most of your income traveling, you would not want to have your occupation defined in a way that you would not be considered disabled if you could continue the same kind of work, but be unable to travel. You want your occupation to be defined in terms of how you actually make your money. If that is not possible, you want the definition of your occupation to be as close as possible to your own occupation.

The second form of limitation on own occupation disability insurance concerns conditions you must meet before you are considered disabled. These conditions are often rather extreme and may require, for example, retraining or extensive physical or other rehabilitation before the insurance company agrees that you can no longer perform your work. The more hurdles you must jump in order to establish that you are disabled, the less assurance you have that you will receive disability payments.

Obtain sufficient coverage to meet your needs

The benefit of disability payments (usually monthly payments) is critical. Of course, the higher the benefit, the higher the premium will be. Try to get sufficient coverage so that together with your other items of income, you will be able to live at a satisfactory minimum standard. Be aware that disability payments are taxable if the premium for the disability insurance policy was paid by your employer or in some other fashion from pre-tax income. On the other hand, disability payments are tax free if they are paid by the policyholder out of after-tax money. In nearly every instance, it is preferable to use after-tax money to purchase disability insurance, so that the payments you receive if you became disabled are tax free.

 Choose a reasonable exclusionary period

The *exclusionary period* is the amount of time you must be disabled before you are eligible for benefits at all. In general, the longer the exclusionary period the smaller the premium. Exclusionary periods of ninety days are typical, but some are shorter and some are longer. Some forms of coverage distinguish short-term (generally up to six months or one year) and long-term (generally up to age 65 or even longer) benefits. If your other sources of income would tide you over for a number of months, and particularly if your employment agreement provides you with a certain amount of compensation for a short time period, you may want to put your limited funds on the long-term disability side.

Choose the duration for which benefits will be paid

You must also look at the duration or period for which benefits will be paid. Some policies pay benefits until a certain age, such as 65, and some pay them for a flat term of years, such as ten years. Some people choose to purchase disability insurance that provides payments until the age of Social Security, which can be as young as age 62.

☑ Be sure that there is coverage for partial disability

A good disability insurance policy should provide you with benefits in the event of *partial disability*. Partial disability is the inability to do some of your work, but not all of it. Many disability policies provide that if you are unable to do a certain amount of work, generally three-quarters of your usual work, you are considered totally disabled and entitled to full benefits.

☑ Be sure your policy contains a waiver of premium provision

A *waiver of premium* provision provides that you do not have to continue making payments for your disability insurance during the time you are disabled. There is generally a slight additional cost for inclusion of such a provision, but it is well worth it.

☑ Be sure the premium is guaranteed for a reasonably long period of time

Be sure that the disability insurance you purchase is the kind that has a *guaranteed renewable* premium. This is a provision that gives you the right to renew your disability insurance policy for a period of time, sometimes as long as ten or twenty years, at premiums that are in effect when you first purchase the policy. The period of time should in no event be less than five years. You certainly do not want to buy a good disability insurance policy and then be unable to renew it because the company has raised your premium beyond your ability to pay.

Be sure that the period of contestability is two years or less

The *period of contestability* is the period within which the insurance company may challenge the validity of your application and deny your claim if something is incorrect. Since disability policies are based on representations that are made by the person obtaining the insurance, there is always the possibility of a challenge to your representations at a later time. You should be absolutely sure when you file your application that every representation you make is complete and correct, particularly those pertaining to your health and medical history. Nevertheless, you want there to be a time after which the issue is closed. The time period is frequently twenty-four months.

 Obtain a full copy of your disability insurance policy

Like with any insurance policy, it is important that you have a complete copy of the policy and that you keep it in a place where you or others can access it should you need to do so.

• • • • •

Making a Claim for Disability Benefits

If you are unfortunate enough to suffer an illness or injury that entitles you to disability benefits, you must be very serious about making your claim. The first thing you should do is read your insurance policy carefully to be certain that you do precisely what it indicates. Insurance companies are not anxious to pay disability benefits and you do not want to give your insurance company an excuse for delaying. The second thing you should do is get proper documentation from your doctors, therapists, and employer. Since you are telling your disability insurance company that you are not able to perform your work because of an illness or injury, you must be prepared to prove it.

Insurance companies will always require you to provide certain information to them and to consent to letting them contact other people such as your doctor or employer. You will be required to complete and sign forms for these purposes. Prepare these people for such contacts by letting them know what you are doing and what you have advised the insurance company.

Be sure to keep a file of every document and letter that you send or receive in regard to a disability claim. You will need these materials as the matter progresses. Do not be surprised if once you have filed a disability claim, you receive a telephone call from someone in the insurance company asking to visit with you. This is an appropriate request and you should respond to it by scheduling the visit and fully advising the representative who visits you about your condition and its impact on your work.

Section IV

The Lessons

Resolving Problems

CHAPTER 10

Buying Goods and Services

Unfortunately, the contracts pertaining to most of the goods and services you will purchase in your life are not negotiable. When you buy things in a store or order them from a catalog, you can make whatever selection you like but you cannot change the terms of sale of anything that you are buying. This is also true for the guarantees and warranties that come with most goods and services. The reason that sellers of many things provide you with what is known as a limited warranty is that this term gives them a legal leg up when you realize later that the warranty only applies to parts but not service, that the warranty only lasts for a brief period of time, or that the warranty requires you to deliver the item to some remote place. If you read limited warranties carefully (which many people do not do until the product or service proves defective), you will see that most of them are pretty close to worthless.

In those situations when you are really able to negotiate a contract for goods or services, there are specific items you should address. Some of these pertain to the goods and services themselves and some pertain to the guarantees or warranties that are provided with them. Although these contracts will surely be a small percentage of your total contracts for goods and services, they will probably be the most important ones. For example, you can sometimes bargain about the guarantee on a used automobile. You can always bargain about the terms of a contract to make significant improvements or repairs to your house. In some instances, you cannot bargain about the terms of specific contracts, but you can choose from among several contracts with different terms. For these situations, it is important to know what to look for in contracts for goods and services and the guarantees and warranties that go with them.

Checklist for What a Contract to Buy Goods should Include

- ❏ Precisely what you are buying
- ❏ The price and terms of payment
- ❏ Where and when the goods will be delivered
- ❏ All promises on which you are relying
- ❏ Statement that the sale is subject to whatever guarantee or warranty is being provided
- ❏ If the goods are provided *to your satisfaction* or you are receiving an approval period
- ❏ If there is any regulatory or insurance standard to be satisfied

☑ Precisely what you are buying

This is particularly important when you are buying something unique, such as a musical instrument or something like an item of custom woodwork. If you are buying a specific item, the contract should describe it as precisely as possible. Include serial numbers, colors, year of manufacture, and other characteristics that unmistakably identify the item you are buying. If you are buying several items, the contract should specify precisely how many.

If the contract is for one or more items that you have not yet examined, particularly items that are being custom made, it should describe the quality of the major component or components of the item. If the item is custom-made out of wood, for example, the contract should specify the type of wood, the grade, and the finish. If a particular finish, such as a particular paint or varnish, is to be provided, the contract should say that. If loose items are to be sold with the major item—such as, for example, chairs, life preservers, or storage facilities on a boat—these should be specifically mentioned. If spare parts are to be provided, these should also be specifically mentioned.

 The price and terms of payment

This is obvious, but often not taken seriously enough. For example, if you are agreeing to pay one-half of the cost of goods before they are delivered and one-half upon delivery, the contract should say that. If you are agreeing to a certain amount of time for payment, the contract should say that. Generally, if a contract says nothing about the time of payment, it is assumed that payment is due in full upon delivery of the goods. Be sure that the contract says that any deposit you pay for goods you have ordered is credited to the purchase price.

 Where and when the goods will be delivered

When a contract says something like *F.O.B. Albany, New York*, it means that the goods will be placed on a common carrier at Albany, New York, but you will be responsible for shipment costs and risks thereafter. If the contract uses initials or terms you are not familiar with, make sure you get an explanation of what they mean and how they affect your agreement. If you expect the item to be delivered to your home or office, the contract should specifically say so.

The contract should state the date by which the goods will be delivered. Many contracts allow a grace period for late delivery and provide that if the goods are not delivered by the end of the grace period, the contract is void. Since no one wants to wait forever for something that has been ordered, this is an important provision.

All promises on which you are relying

Most contracts contain near the end what is known as an *integration clause*. This is a clause that says that there are no promises other than those stated in the contract, and oral representations may not be relied upon. Even if a contract does not contain such a provision, there are various legal arguments against the existence of promises outside the contract. Therefore, if you are relying on such a promise, have it included specifically in the written contract.

Statement that the sale is subject to whatever guarantee or warranty is being provided

The subject of guarantees or warranties requires further explanation, as begins on page 237.

If the goods are provided to your satisfaction or you are receiving an approval period

The right to return goods no questions asked is a very useful right to have when you are purchasing goods, but it must be made clear. It is important that a time period be indicated for approval or a trial period. The contract should state that you will receive a full refund of the purchase price if you exercise the right to return the goods.

If there is any regulatory or insurance standard to be satisfied

Some products, such as electrical products, must satisfy building codes and various insurance underwriting standards. If you are buying custom-made goods falling within any such category, be sure your contract indicates that the goods will satisfy the required standards.

· · · · ·

Contract to Buy Services

The services you will be acquiring may cover a wide range. Some services call for physical work, such as repairs and improvements to houses and cars, and some call for personal interactions, such as teaching and professional advice. For this reason, contracts for services tend to be individualized, but there are some common aspects to them.

Checklist for Contract to Buy Services

- ❏ Be sure the services you are buying are fully described
- ❏ Be sure the price of the services should be precisely specified
- ❏ Be sure the sales contract includes proper insurance requirements
- ❏ Be sure the sales contract includes any guarantee that is being provided
- ❏ Be sure that the sales contract so provides if the service you are buying must satisfy a regulatory or insurance requirement

☑ Be sure the services you are buying are fully described

Services are often harder to describe than products. There are two basic ways to describe them—specification and performance. A *specification* contract details precisely what will be done, but not the result of the work. A *performance* contract describes the result of the work. For example, a landscaping contract could say that two people will be provided next Thursday for six hours of lawn and garden work. A performance contract for the same purpose could say that next Thursday all of your grass will be cut, all of your trees will be pruned of dead limbs, and all of your flower beds will be fertilized. From the point of view of a consumer, a performance contract is almost always preferable because if lets you know in advance how much you will be paying to accomplish particular things.

 Be sure the price of the services should be precisely specified

If you are using a performance contract, this is not usually a worrisome matter. If you are using a specification contract, however, you must be sure that the contract establishes a price for any additional work that may be needed to accomplish your purpose. It is best if the contract requires payment upon completion of certain amounts of work, so that you will be able to approve the work before payment.

 Be sure the sales contract includes proper insurance requirements

Whenever work is being done on property that you own, such as your house, or involves anything of danger to other people or their property, the service provider must be properly insured. Contractors are accustomed to providing copies of their insurance certificate to potential customers and you should feel free to ask for one if there is any doubt about the matter. Even though common sense and frequently state law require insurance for many forms of service, contractors sometimes fail to obtain it.

 Be sure the sales contract includes any guarantee that is being provided

Some guarantees and warranties concern matters involving both a service and a product. For example, roofers guarantee their workmanship and also provide customers with the manufacturer's guarantee for the roofing materials, such as shingles.

Some guarantees have time limits. Make sure the limits are long enough to determine if the service and possibly a product that go with it are satisfactory. For example, garden companies often guarantee that plantings will live for a certain amount of time. Whatever guarantee you intend to receive, be sure that it is referred to in the contract.

 Be sure that the sales contract so provides if the service you are buying must satisfy a regulatory or insurance requirement

Many expensive services must satisfy strict regulatory and insurance requirements. For example, hookups to public utilities are strictly regulated. Fencing must carefully follow property lines, be of legal height, and meet other requirements for certain purposes such as with swimming pools. Construction work must be in compliance with various building codes in order for insurance to be obtained to cover it. If you are purchasing a service and possibly the product as well that must meet such requirements, be certain that your contract indicates that it will meet them.

Many of the contracts for special goods and services you may buy will be printed on forms of the manufacturer or contractor. Provided that they cover the necessary matters, there is no problem with such forms. A lengthy contract is not required for most purposes and, in fact, many such agreements are provided by letter. At the end of this chapter, sample letters for the purchase of goods and services are provided.

• • • • •

Guarantees and Warranties

Since the true value of the goods and services you purchase depends to a great extent upon the assurances you receive from the seller, you should look carefully at those assurances whenever you are buying something. Unfortunately, an increasing number of guarantees and warranties have no real value because they are limited in some manner that prevents you from relying upon them when you need them. The following checklist will help you determine whether the guarantee or warranty you are receiving with a product or service is of real value to you.

Checklist for Guarantees and Warranties

- ❏ Be sure that the guarantee or warranty you are receiving is adequate
- ❏ Be sure the guarantees or warranties state what will be done if the product or service fails
- ❏ Do not accept guarantees that have requirements you cannot satisfy
- ❏ Be sure the guarantees and warranties cover regulatory and insurance requirements you must satisfy

☑ Be sure that the guarantee or warranty you are receiving is adequate

For these purposes, the legal differences between guarantees and warranties are not important. What is important is that whatever you are receiving assures you of the satisfactoriness of the goods or services for a reasonable amount of time without much additional expenditure on your part. A guarantee on the *power train* of a used car does you almost no good at all, since you can bet that whatever causes the car to break down every two miles will not be considered by the dealer to be part of the power train. A 30-day guarantee on a plumbing job in your house does not do you much good either. As a general rule, such jobs begin leaking on about the 32nd day! To be effective, a guarantee or warranty should give you a reasonable assurance that if anything is seriously wrong with the goods or services you are buying, you will be able to rely on the seller for replacements or repairs.

 Be sure the guarantees or warranties state what will be done if the product or service fails

If a manufacturer promises to replace a product that fails within a certain amount of time, the guarantee or warranty should state that. If a contractor assures it will perform repair work at no cost to you for at least three years, the guarantee should state that.

People who sell products and services often tell customers that, for one reason or another, they cannot put certain things in writing in a guarantee or warranty, but they will abide by them. Do not consider accepting such an assurance. Whatever prevents the seller of goods or services from stating something in a guarantee or warranty, you can bet will prevent him or her from honoring any oral promise made if push comes to shove. As a legal matter, you will be stuck with whatever appears in writing and nothing more.

 Do not accept guarantees that have requirements you cannot satisfy

If your large screen television is reasonably guaranteed, but you must deliver it at your expense to some place 1,000 miles away to get it repaired, forget it. This is the sort of guarantee that is worthless, because you need to do something ridiculously inconvenient and expensive to exercise it. As a general rule, product guarantees should be enforceable by a customer with minimal expense and difficulty. Service guarantees should require the service provider to provide the repair services in the same manner as the original services.

☑ Be sure the guarantees and warranties cover regulatory and insurance requirements you must satisfy

If you have purchased something that must satisfy a public or insurance requirement in order to be used, be sure that the guarantee promises that the product will continue to meet that requirement. For example, if you hire a contractor to install a fireplace in your house and the fireplace breaks in a way that causes it to no longer satisfy state or insurance requirements, you have purchased a decorative fireplace. If this was your intention, no problem, but if you wanted the real thing, you would not have it. If someone you are planning to buy something from does not want to guarantee adherence to state and insurance requirements, it is a safe bet that he or she does not know those requirements or is not adhering to them. Do not deal with such a person.

In addition to different kinds of short forms, sellers of goods and services often use simple letters as a means of confirming their contracts with customers. If such a letter covers the matters you need, it is perfectly satisfactory. If not, you will need to discuss changes with the person with whom you are dealing. In the event you wish to prepare such a letter agreement yourself, it should generally follow the following format.

Sample Letter to Someone Who is Selling Goods to You

September 1, 2005

Mr. Joel Kitridge
President
Widget Manufacturing Company
30750 Industrial Boulevard
Terre Haute, Indiana 00000

Dear Mr. Kitridge:
This letter will confirm my order from your company of two custom-made widgets, model x-1000. The price for the two widgets will be $1,260.58. A 10% deposit to be credited against the purchase price is enclosed. The widgets will be prepared in accordance with the specifications in your July 2005 catalog and both of them will be blue. The widgets will be delivered to my home at the address below, not later than October 1, 2005, at your company's expense. The widgets will be accompanied by a guarantee assuring me of any necessary repairs or replacements for a period of one year, at no expense to me. If repairs and/or replacements are necessary, they will be accomplished at your dealership in this city.

If this letter correctly states our agreement, please sign one of the copies I have furnished and return it to me.

Thank you for your assistance.

Sincerely,
Darlene Smithson
4206 Clovetree Drive
Atlanta, Georgia 00000

Enclosures

Agreed and accepted this ____ day of _____, 2005
Widget Manufacturing Company
By:_____
Joel Kitridge, President

Sample Letter to Someone Who is Providing Services to You

July 24, 2005

Ms. Marjorie Montana
Expressions Window Treatments
342 St. Margaret Lane
York, Pennsylvania 00000

Dear Ms. Montana:
This letter will confirm my purchase from your company of custom-made curtains for the living room and master bedroom of our house. Both sets of curtains will be made out of fabric number DC-2901 from the catalog you showed me and my husband and backed with suitable backing to keep out all light. The curtains will be custom-fitted and installed not later than September 15, 2005. They will be guaranteed against shrinkage and discoloration for a period of two years from the date of installation. Our understanding is that we will pay one-half of the $1,760 charge for these curtains at the time of this order, and the remaining one-half when satisfactory installation is complete.

If this letter correctly states our agreement, please sign one of the copies I have furnished and return it to me.

Thank you for your assistance.

Sincerely,
Barbara Pearson
2839 Willow Brook Circle
York, Pennsylvania 00000

Enclosure
Agreed and accepted this _____ day of _____, 2005
Expressions Window Treatments
By:_____
Marjorie Montana

It is important when you write such letters that you enclose a copy for the other person to sign and return to you. As long as you have covered the matters that are necessary, letters like this are fully binding contracts.

CHAPTER 11

Resolving Disputes

Before turning to the subject of resolving disputes, it is important to discuss ways to avoid disputes. Some people seem to have a knack for not doing some pretty simple things that keep other people out of trouble. Unless you enjoy long and antagonistic disputes that could have been avoided—in which case, you are a very unusual person—it will be worth your time to review the checklist of easy steps that will keep you out of difficulty a lot of the time. For the most part, these steps are what you would do if you used common sense. The problem is that many people do not use common sense when it comes to disputes.

Checklist of Ways to Avoid Disputes

- ❏ Retain copies of your important documents
- ❏ Open all bank statements, bills, and other business mail promptly after you receive them
- ❏ Do not discuss disputes with people who are not working for you
- ❏ Answer correspondence and telephone calls
- ❏ Do not contact a lawyer except as a last resort
- ❏ Do not sweat the little things

☑ Retain copies of your important documents

Having the right documents easily available does several essential things. First, it gives you airtight proof of whatever the document shows. If the document is some sort of contract like a bill of sale or a warranty, nothing else proves what the contract says. If the document commemorates information you or someone else has, nothing does it better. If the document is like an insurance policy and tells you what you need to do to take action such as making a claim, you can lose the whole matter by not following it. And you can be sure of this—the businesses and agencies you have to wrestle with have copies of every important document easily available to them. Your HMO has a copy of your provider agreement and the IRS has a copy of your last tax return.

In order to keep all of your documents organized and available, you need to do exactly one thing. Obtain a cardboard box known as a banker's or file box that you can purchase at any variety store, a box of manila folders, preferably legal length since some documents are longer than 8½ x 11, and a cheap ballpoint pen. Write something on the label space on the outside of the box, so you do not forget what the box contains. Write on the manila folders things like *car insurance policy, past years' tax returns, receipts for 2004 car expenses, warranties for house appliances*, and so forth. When you receive a document such as an addendum or letter that relates to one of the folders, just stick it in it. You will never need to do anything else to keep records and you will not spend the rest of your life trying to figure out where they are. You will also make the life of your tax preparer a lot easier at tax time.

☑ Open all bank statements, bills, and other business mail promptly after you receive them

Many contracts with banks, credit card companies, and others with whom you deal state specifically that you must notify the company within a certain period of time of an error or you lose the right to complain about it. In the case of bank statements, this process is called *reconciling*. Since every company makes mistakes from time to time and since identity theft is becoming easier and more frequent, prompt review of these items is increasingly important. When you find an error of some kind, report it immediately and, if there is any question about your report, send a letter confirming it.

 Do not discuss disputes with people who are not working for you

If you have a car accident, for example, do not talk to the other person's insurance company or the other person's lawyer. If you are having a dispute about a defective item or poor service, do not talk to anyone who might want to do the seller of that item or service a favor. Even if you feel sure you could speak with people who are not on your side without saying anything damaging to your position, you may be surprised to learn that you have made a mistake or the other person has taken your remarks out of context.

As a general rule when you are having a dispute, speak only with people on your side, such as your insurance company or its representatives or people you are required to speak with, such as police officers. The only exception to this is when the other person is truly trying to settle the matter with you. When lawyers have discussions to settle matters, they agree that the discussions are off the record. This is a good idea for laymen as well.

 Answer correspondence and telephone calls

People who study hundreds and thousands of disputes always conclude that people who make themselves inaccessible get into far more trouble than those who do not. People hate being avoided, especially when they feel they have been done an injustice. Most people think that anyone who becomes unavailable when the going gets rough is probably blameworthy in some respect.

✅ Do not contact a lawyer except as a last resort

Lawyers should be used for matters that are reasonably large and serious. You would be foolish not to use a lawyer if all else failed and you needed to get your health insurer to authorize a critical operation for you or a family member. You would be foolish not to use a lawyer if you were seriously injured in an accident caused by someone else or if you were sued for a significant amount of money for something you allegedly did. But for most of the situations that people face there is a reasonable choice about whether to use a lawyer.

There are at least three good reasons to avoid using a lawyer whenever possible.

First, even the gentlest lawyer in the world ratchets the matter up a notch. When someone uses a lawyer, the person on the other end either feels at a disadvantage or goes out and gets his or her own lawyer. If the person at the other end is with a large company or the government, he or she already has lawyers waiting in the wings. Partly because of their adversarial nature and partly because some lawyers need a good fight to show they are brave soldiers, involving lawyers in a dispute will often turn a lukewarm disagreement into an angry and costly battle.

Second, the introduction of lawyers in a matter involving someone else usually changes future dealings with that person forever. If your dispute is with someone you may be dealing with at a later date, a good way to sour the relationship is to use a lawyer when you do not have to. Even if your dispute is with a cold-blooded party like a bank or insurance company, you may still want to leave the person-to-person door open for the future. Business files often keep records of people who involve lawyers in different matters and other people may see those records at later times.

Third, lawyers are expensive in more ways than one. Obviously lawyers charge fees for their services, one way or the other. In addition to this, dealing with lawyers takes a good deal of time. Lawyers work on all sorts of deadlines even when they are not in court. For the most part, clients must fit into those deadlines, since lawyers cannot do very much about them.

 Do not sweat the little things
The saying *It's not about money, it's about principle* loses its punch in the eighteenth month of a dispute that has proven to be ten times as time-consuming and expensive as it was ever worth in the first place. When you are headed into a long and costly dispute on principle, either take a cold shower and go out to dinner or write the other person the strongest possible letter telling him or her how you feel and then throw it away. When there is no payoff at the end, any dispute-resolution process becomes overwhelmingly aggravating and tedious.

· · · · ·

Handling Legal Disputes
It is impossible these days to avoid having legal disputes from time to time. People who sell you things or perform services will sometimes give you defective items or perform unsatisfactory work. Difficulties of one sort or another will arise with your apartment or house. Banks and credit card companies will screw up your accounts from time to time and, on top of this, all of the government agencies you would like to rely upon will botch up a lot of things themselves. Some people spend most of their time haggling with people about these things

or, in these days of dialing menus and Internet sites, trying to figure out who to haggle with. If you would prefer to do something else with your life, there are a number of ways to resolve nearly all of these disputes without spending money or considerable time doing so.

Although other methods such as requesting the assistance of a public agency or filing a suit in court are available for resolving disputes, most disputes do not justify the time, effort, and possible expense these things require. If you have a substantial claim against you, such as concerning your car, apartment, or house, it should be covered by your insurance. If you have a substantial claim against someone else, you should be able to get a competent attorney to handle it on a contingent fee basis. A *contingent fee arrangement* is one in which your lawyer gets paid a percentage of what you recover in damages. For most disputes of small or moderate size, a properly prepared letter will usually get you to an acceptable result in reasonably short time.

Anyone can write a properly prepared legal dispute letter by using the checklist that follows. You will be amazed how easy it is to use such letters effectively. Each item on the checklist is important and you should follow it carefully. If you need a little help writing this type of letter, ask someone for it. Unless you enjoy speaking to someone in New Delhi or Manila after holding on the phone for forty-five minutes, do not waste a lot of time trying to resolve disputes before writing the letter.

Checklist for Writing a Legal Letter

☐ Type your letter
☐ Use proper (but not fancy) English and proper punctuation and spelling
☐ Address your letter to a precise individual if possible
☐ Send your letter by CERTIFIED MAIL, RETURN RECEIPT REQUESTED unless you are personally acquainted with the person you are writing to, such as a neighbor or relative
☐ Review the facts of the matter accurately at the beginning of your letter
☐ Tell the person receiving the letter precisely what you want him or her to do
☐ State your reasons for being entitled to what you want
☐ Give the other person a time limit for resolving the matter
☐ End your letter by stating that if you do not receive what you are demanding, you will *pursue appropriate legal action*
☐ Do not say things that can only make the matter worse for you

✔ Type your letter
If you do not have a typewriter or computer, borrow one. If you do not know how to use one, get someone to type your letter for you. Businesses and public agencies do not take handwritten letters seriously, even if they can read them.

✔ Use proper (but not fancy) English and proper punctuation and spelling
Fancy language and legalese are not important when you are trying to resolve a dispute. What is important is that your letter looks like it was

prepared by someone who is dead serious and knows what is going on. People who receive legal letters ask themselves only one question—*Do I have to respond to this person?* If the answer is no, the letter goes in the circular file under the desk. If the answer is yes, the next question is, *What do I have to do to get rid of him or her?*

☑ Address your letter to a precise individual if possible
Letters have a lot more force when they arrive in someone's own name. Be sure to get the spelling and title of the person correct. If you are unable to get the name of a precise person by looking through papers or making some phone calls, address your letter to someone in the correct capacity, such as *Customer Relations Manager.* Letters addressed *Dear Sir/Madam*: should be the last choice.

☑ Send your letter by CERTIFIED MAIL, RETURN RECEIPT REQUESTED unless you are personally acquainted with the person you are writing to, such as a neighbor or relative
Do not use faxes or email for letters intended to resolve legal disputes.

People do not take such correspondence as seriously as letters received in the mail. Certified mail, return receipt requested, is particularly effective for two reasons. The person receiving the letter knows you spent money by going to the post office and, thus, you are serious. This person also knows you have evidence that he or she received it because it had to be signed for in the presence of a postal worker.

☑ Review the facts of the matter accurately at the beginning of your letter
If you are complaining about something the other person did or failed to do, get the dates and other specific facts such as names exactly right. This shows the person receiving the letter that you are serious and

ready for further action if necessary. Do not include unnecessary facts in your letter, since they confuse the matter and weaken your letter.

☑ Tell the person receiving the letter precisely what you want him or her to do

If you want an insurance company to pay a claim in a certain amount, say it. If you want an automobile repair company to correct an improper repair, say it. If you want a bank or credit card company to get off your back about an incorrect charge, say it. Once you have received the attention of the other person, you do not want him or her to be guessing what you want to happen. Most companies want to know immediately what it will take to get rid of you.

☑ State your reasons for being entitled to what you want

If you are making a claim under some sort of guarantee, identify the guarantee and quote a few relevant words from it. If you are making a claim under a contract of some sort, do the same thing. You can enclose copies of small documents such as bills of sale or receipts, to strengthen your letter. People who receive letters that refer to or enclose documents are always impressed with the seriousness of the writer and his or her ability to carry through.

If you have learned something useful from a state agency or spoken with someone with relevant knowledge about the matter in dispute, state that in your letter. If a public agency tells you that a particular fact is useful or someone respected in a particular field confirms your judgment about the particular matter, that is always useful. Most people who receive complaints do not want word of their shortcomings to get around. When another person is in the picture, most of these people happily wrap the matter up.

✓ Give the other person a time limit for resolving the matter

A lot of the people involved in legal disputes would just as soon let them go on forever. For you, however, the idea is to get the dispute over as quickly as possible and get on with your life. Therefore, you should give the other party a reasonable amount of time to conclude the matter, but not excessive time. For most disputes, it is reasonable to expect a reply, one way or the other, within a week or two.

✓ End your letter by stating that if you do not receive what you are demanding, you will pursue appropriate legal action

Using the words *pursue appropriate legal action* gives you all the clout you can get without requiring you to figure out precisely what legal action would be appropriate and how you will take it. (If the legal action that is appropriate is clearly established, such as where an HMO provider agreement states how a member must appeal denials of coverage, you may state that you will take that action.) Appropriate legal action may sometimes be a lawsuit and sometimes other steps. You may or may not need a lawyer for various forms of appropriate legal action, but if you write legal letters correctly, you should not have to worry about that in most instances.

✓ Do not say things that can only make the matter worse for you

Do not threaten any form of legal action other than *appropriate legal action* or filing a lawsuit. Specifically, do not threaten to report the other person to any form of public agency. There are many times when you are fully justified in using the help of a public agency, but the law does not allow you to threaten it. Do not make personal remarks about the other person or anyone associated with him or her.

Legal disputes involve money or things that can be valued in money. If the other person is the most offensive human being on earth, keep it to yourself. Also, do not impugn the integrity of the other person's business. There may be a thousand disputes of the same sort as yours, but the purpose of your letter is to resolve your dispute and get on with it. Remarks about people or their businesses can get you into trouble and never help to put a dispute behind you.

The following are various sample letters you can use to resolve a dispute. Tailor the letters to your specific need following the steps provided.

Sample Letter Regarding Defective Repairs

100 Oliver Way
Terre Haute, Indiana 00000
May 17, 2005

CERTIFIED MAIL
RETURN RECEIPT REQUESTED

Mr. Harold C. Williams
Acme Repair Company
150 W. Maple Lane
Terre Haute, Indiana 00000

Dear Mr. Williams:
On May 8, 2005, I telephoned your company to request repair of our Westinghouse dishwasher. Two service personnel from your company came to our house on May 10, 2005, and stated that they repaired the dishwasher, which was leaking whenever it ran. A copy of the bill for those services, which the men left with us, is enclosed. On May 12, 2005, the dishwasher started leaking again. I have telephoned your business three times since that occurred and requested that the matter be repaired. As you know, the bill received from you indicates that all repairs are warrantied for 30 days.

I insist that you either repair the dishwasher properly immediately or return to me the amount of your bill ($174.26) so that I may use the money to have repairs made properly. If this fails to occur within the next 10 days, I will pursue appropriate legal action.

Sincerely,
Michael Washburn

Enclosure

Sample Letter to Bank Regarding Checking Account

25 Wisconsin Avenue
Schenectady, New York 00000

May 20, 2005

CERTIFIED MAIL
RETURN RECEIPT REQUESTED

Mr. Melvin T. Handscum
Manager
Round The World Bank
1000 Main Street
Schenectady, New York 00000

Re: Account No. 1234 5678 9

Dear Mr. Handscum:
I have maintained the above checking account with your bank for the past six years. On my statement of February this year, two checks that I did not write were debited. I telephoned and advised one of your employees of the error on March 7, 2005. Since that time, I have received statements for March and April, neither of which reflects an appropriate correction. The result is that the balance maintained in my account is erroneous and insufficient for my payment of bills.

I do not understand why this matter has not been corrected, but I cannot wait any longer for that to occur. I am afraid that your failure to correct this matter will result in my bouncing checks inadvertently, which will cause difficulty and embarrassment for me. I have been advised by the State Banking Commission that it maintains a procedure to remedy difficulties of this nature, and I will utilize that procedure if necessary. I would appreciate your remedying this matter immediately to avoid my having to take appropriate legal action.

Sincerely,
Sylvia T. Jennings

Sample Letter Requesting Approval to See a Specialist

227 Melon Street
Seattle, Washington 00000

May 15, 2005

CERTIFIED MAIL
RETURN RECEIPT REQUESTED

Ms. Georgia W. Caldwell
Account Manager
Heritage Health Management Organization
10347 Gateway Drive
Seattle, Washington 00000

Re: Member No. 34679-0

Dear Ms. Caldwell:
I am a member of your HMO and my general physician is Dr. Seymour J. Fishman. I have been utilizing Dr. Fishman since my enrollment as a member of your HMO in January, 1998.

For the past six months, I have been consulting Dr. Fishman concerning severe pain in my left hip, which is apparently degenerating. Specifically, I visited Dr. Fishman on November 27, 2004, January 18, 2005, and April 3, 2005. On each occasion, Dr. Fishman prescribed medicine intended to relieve the pain I was experiencing, but took no further steps. I believe that my left hip is seriously degenerated and I have requested on numerous occasions that Dr. Fishman refer me to an orthopedic specialist for consultation concerning this matter. Dr. Fishman advised me that you have declined to authorize such a referral.

My provider agreement with your HMO states in paragraph XVII that referral when necessary to a suitable specialist will take place. Clearly, referral of me to an orthopedic specialist is necessary at this time and your failure to refer me to a specialist is a violation of our contract. In addition, your actions are jeopardizing my continued health and causing me considerable pain and discomfort.

I request that you authorize Dr. Fishman to make immediate arrangements for me to be referred to a suitable orthopedic specialist. If this does not occur, I intend to follow the procedures set forth in the provider agreement to seek a review of this matter with your Review Board and, if necessary, with the State Health Commission. I would like to avoid the necessity for taking these steps, but your actions are causing continued injury to my health and well-being.

I would like to hear from you within one week of this date, since this matter is urgent.

Sincerely,
Robert O. Barnett

Sample Letter Regarding Lack of Trash Removal Services

2963 Evergreen Drive
Peoria, Illinois 00000

April 30, 2005

CERTIFIED MAIL
RETURN RECEIPT REQUESTED

Mr. Barkley Broadfoot
Superintendent
Essex County Health Department
379 Stone Hill Lane
Peoria, Illinois 00000

Dear Mr. Broadfoot:
My husband and I reside at 2963 Evergreen Drive in Peoria, Illinois. This is within the sanitation district under your authority. We are supposed to receive trash removal services twice a week and, for the past three months, have been receiving those services only once per week. I telephoned your offices on March 13, 2005 and spoke with Mr. Green concerning this matter, and on April 17, 2005 I spoke with Ms. Patridge concerning it. Nothing has been done in response to these conversations.

I request that the service to which we are entitled be resumed immediately. If not, my husband and I will take appropriate legal action to have this reviewed by the appropriate authority. As taxpayers and residents of your district, we are not receiving these services to which we are entitled.

Sincerely,
Carol P. Applebee

Conclusion

You are now ready to face the legal matters that arise in your life with the confidence that you can handle them in a way that serves your interests. The knowledge you have received in this book is sufficient so that you can face the tasks and documents you need to rent an apartment or buy a house, buy a car, obtain medical care and insurance, pay taxes, deal with your employment, and manage your finances.

You must be sure when you are working with these matters that you ask all the questions you need to ask to be certain that each item is taken care of the way you intend. If you are talking to a landlord or broker about your apartment lease, do not be afraid to ask, *Are there any charges in this lease besides the deposit and base monthly rent?* If you are buying a term life insurance policy to provide expenses for a child in case you die in the next ten years, do not be reluctant to ask the broker or agent, *How long does this policy give me the absolute right to renew it and what is the cost?*

In some of the things you will do, like working out your medical care coverage or buying a house, you will have lots of questions. Be sure to get answers to all of them and ask the person you are dealing with to point out the particular provisions of the document you will need to sign. Do not let anyone tell you that you are being too fussy or taking too much time. When your life and your money are involved, no one has the right to tell you this.

I hope that this book will make it easier for you to manage your affairs in a difficult world. If I could make banks and insurance companies and everyone who sells things to you considerate and fair-minded, I would love to do so. Since that is not possible, however, I have tried in this book to do the next best thing—to give you the ability when handling your legal affairs to accomplish your goals and to avoid any pitfalls.

I am certain this is possible and I wish you success.

Index

401(k) plans, 45

A

A.M. Best's, 97, 213
accidents, 119, 120, 121, 122, 125
  checklist for handling, 119
adjustable rate mortgage (ARM), 133, 137
annual leave, 6, 7, 9, 11, 12
annual percentage rate (APR), 42, 110
apartments
  complaints about, 90
    checklist for, 91
    sample letter, 92, 93
  defining the essentials, 80
  finding an, 79, 81, 82
    checklist for, 80
  insurance, 95, 164
    checklist for, 97
    making a claim under, 98
      checklist for, 99
      sample letter, 101, 102
    terms used in, 96
  renting an, 79
  sample letter regarding lack of trash removal services, 259
approved provider, 175
at-will employment, 4, 6
ATM receipts, 39, 41
audit, 53
automobiles, 103
  checklist for buying, 107
  checklist of costs of owning, 104
  insurance, 107, 109, 113, 114, 115, 161, 164
    checklist of components of, 115
  price, 104, 105

B

bank statements, 43, 245, 246
  reconciling, 39, 41
banking
  terms used in, 42
beneficiary, 207
benefit period, 219
benefits, 6, 7, 8, 11, 207
  checklist of, 11
bills, 30, 33
bodily injury liability, 115
borrowing capacity, 207
bounced check, 42
broom clean, 141, 146, 153
building inspection, 137

C

cash surrender value, 207
certificate of deposit (CD), 43
checkbook, 39
checking account, 30, 38
  balance, 42
  checklist of dos and don'ts for, 39
  how to handle, 38
  sample letter regarding, 256
checks, 65, 66
  blank, 39
  completing, 39, 40
  ledgers, 39, 40, 41
  stubs, 39, 41, 65, 66
claims, 99
closing, 126, 131, 135, 136, 137, 140, 142, 143, 145, 147, 149, 150, 152, 155, 156
  checklist for, 153
  costs, 132, 133
  documents, 156, 157
co-pay, 175
collision coverage, 115, 117
commission, 6
  draw, 6
common area, 85
compensation, 24
comprehensive coverage, 115, 117
condominium, 85
cooperative (co-op), 85
covenants, 137, 141
credit, 30, 31, 32, 43
credit cards, 30, 33
credit reports, 32
creditor, 43

D

death, 48
 checklist of things to do to provide for possible, 48
debit card, 43
debtor, 43
deductible, 96, 97, 98, 175
deductions, 6, 53, 66
deeds, 137, 141, 145, 152, 153, 154
deeds of trust, 137, 152
defined benefit plans, 45, 46
demised premises, 85
dependent, 53
deposit slips, 39, 41
deposits, 39, 43
direct deposit, 43
disability, 48
 checklist of things to do to provide for possible, 48
disability insurance, 11, 12, 24, 26, 207, 215
 checklist for obtaining, 221-224
 checklist of possible sources of money, 216
 how to obtain, 220
 making a claim for benefits, 226
 terms used in, 219
discrimination, 8, 21
dispute resolution, 182, 196, 197, 245
 checklist of ways to avoid disputes, 245, 246, 247, 248, 249
documentary stamps, 137
double indemnity, 208
down payment, 110, 137
drug programs, 181

E

emergency road service coverage, 115, 118
emergency services, 180
employee handbooks, 5, 15, 20
employees, 3, 6
 checklist for new, 15
 paperwork for new, 14
 rights as, 15, 20, 22, 23
employer, 6
employer-employee relationship, 4
employment benefits. *See benefits*

employment contracts, 3, 4
 checklist for, 7
 terms used in, 6
ending employment,
 checklist for, 24
enrolled agent, 53, 70
Equifax Credit Information Services, Inc., 31
escrow agent, 137
eviction, 85
exclusionary period, 224
exemption, 53, 56
expenses, 6, 11, 13, 104, 106, 126, 129
Experian, 31
extension, 53
 term, 6, 85

F

Families U.S.A. Foundation, 184
Federal Insurance Contributions Act (FICA), 53, 58, 171
fee, 43
finances, 29
 checklist for managing, 30
financing, 107-111, 126, 132-135, 156
financing commitment, 137
financing condition, 141, 145
fixed rate mortgage, 138
fixtures, 138
flexible spending accounts, 14
floater coverage, 96
for cause, 6

G

gatekeeper, 175
goods, 231
 approval, 234
 checklist for what a contract to buy should include, 232
 delivery, 232, 233
 sample letter, 241
 terms, 232, 233
guaranteed renewable disability policy, 219

H

health clubs, 13
health maintenance organizations (HMOs), 169, 171, 172, 173
  checklist for forming a relationship with, 189
  checklist for obtaining specialists, testing, drugs, and other medical care, 192–196
    sample letter requesting approval to see a specialist, 257
  checklist for resolving disputes with, 198–202, 205
    sample letter, 202
  financial strength, 185
  selecting, 174
    checklist of factors to consider, 176, 177, 178, 180
  state history, 184
  terms used in, 175
  worksheet for comparing, 188
homeowners insurance, 126, 136, 138, 140, 143, 147, 149, 150, 151, 152, 164
  checklist for, 149
houses
  additional insured, 137
  checklist for buying, 126
  contract to buy, 139, 141, 143
    checklist for , 140
  improvements, 138
  insurance, 126, 131
  locations, 126, 127
  points, 138
  repairs, 157, 158
  terms used in buying, 137
HUD-1, 138

I

income taxes, 53, 54, 55
  points, 54
  terms used in, 53
  graduated, 54, 57
independent contractors, 3
independent insurance brokers, 97, 149, 150, 209, 212, 213, 214, 221, 222

individual retirement account (IRA), 45, 46
inspections, 104, 107, 108, 111, 113, 126, 131, 140, 143, 144, 152
  checklist for car, 112
insurance commission, 99, 102
insurance companies, 97
insured person, 208
interest, 43
Internal Revenue Service (IRS), 54
  dealing with the, 74, 75
  Form 1040, 54
  Form 1040A, 54, 65, 66
  Form 1040EZ, 54, 65, 66
  Form 1099, 54, 60, 61, 62, 65, 66, 68
  Form W-2, 54, 60, 61, 62, 65, 66, 68
  Form W-4, 15, 16
  publications, 57
investments, 216

J

job description, 7
job title, 7
joint liability, 30, 34

L

landlord, 86
leases, 80, 82, 84, 86, 87, 90, 95
  assignment, 85
  checklist for, 86
  renewing, 87, 89
  terms used in, 85
legal disputes, 249
  checklist for contract to buy, 252
  checklist for writing a legal letter, 251, 252, 253, 254
  handling, 249, 250
  holding over, 85
level of service, 180
liability insurance, 97, 161–167
  additional coverage, 163, 164
  checklist for obtaining, 163
life insurance, 11, 24, 26, 48, 49, 51, 207
  checklist for purchasing, 209
  tax issues, 210
  terms used in, 207

limits of liability, 96, 175
listing agent, 138
living wills, 48, 50

M

medical care, 169
medical insurance, 11, 24, 25, 26
   checklist of types of, 169
medical records, 189, 190
Medicare, 54, 58, 60, 169, 216
mileage reimbursement, 11, 13
money purchase pension plans, 45, 46
monthly benefit amount, 219
Moody's, 97, 213
mortgages, 138, 152
   guaranty insurance, 138

N

National Association of Health Underwriters, 222
National Committee For Quality Assurance (NCQA), 186
not for cause, 6

O

off-line provider, 175
own occupation disability insurance, 219
owner, 208

P

parking, 104, 107, 109
partial disability, 219, 225
period of contestability, 219, 226
Perkins Loan, 35
permanent illness, 219
personal injury liability, 96
personal injury protection, 115, 118
personal property, 138
personal property rider, 96
physician preferences, 182
point-of-service medical insurance, 169, 170
police reports, 99, 100, 122
policy manuals, 5
powers of attorney, 48, 50

preexisting condition exclusion, 208, 219
preexisting illnesses, 179
preferred provider insurance, 169, 170
premium, 138, 208, 219
preventive services, 180
primary care physician, 198
profit-sharing plans, 45, 46
property damage, 96, 97, 115, 116
provider, 175
provider agreement, 189, 192, 204

R

rating of insurance company, 208, 219
real estate brokers, 80, 81, 86, 87, 89
   dealing with, 82
      checklist for, 83
   selecting, 83
   written contract with, 84
real estate contract, 138, 141, 146, 147
real estate taxes, 126, 129, 130, 136, 138, 140, 142, 152
realtors, 126, 127, 129, 139, 140, 142
recordable form, 139
references, 24, 26, 27
referrals, 175, 193
refund, 54
registration fees, 104
regulatory standards, 232, 234, 235, 237
renewal option, 86
renewal term, 6, 85
renter's insurance. *See insurance*
repairs, 86, 88, 104, 139
   sample letter regarding defective, 255
replacement cost, 100
restrictive covenants, 6, 10, 24, 27, 28
retirement plan, 11, 13, 15, 19, 20, 24, 25, 30, 38, 69
   tax-qualified, 44, 45, 47
   types of, 45
roommates, 94
   checklist for dealing with, 94
   leases, 95
Roth IRA, 46
   rollovers, 47

S

salary, 4, 6, 7, 8, 15, 23
sales contracts, 126, 130
savings, 216
savings certificate, 43
security deposit, 86, 87, 89
services
    checklist for contract to buy, 235, 236
    insurance, 235, 236
    sample letter, 242
settlement sheet, 139, 152, 153, 154
sexual misconduct, 22
shipment costs, 233
sick leave, 6, 7, 9, 11, 12
signatory, 43
Simple plans, 45
simplified employer pension plans (SEP), 45
Social Security, 54, 58, 60, 216
Stafford Loan, 35
Standard and Poor, 97, 213
standard deduction, 55
stop order, 43
student loans, 30, 34, 35, 36
sublease, 86

T

tax bracket, 55
tax credit, 55
tax cycle, 139
tax preparer, 55, 65, 67, 209, 214
    selecting, 69, 70, 71
tax rates, 58
tax returns, 55, 65, 67, 68
    checklist for preparing for, 65
    filing, 63, 64
taxable income, 55
taxes. *See income taxes*
temporary car rental coverage, 115, 118
temporary illness, 220
tenant, 86
term, 4, 6, 21, 86, 220
term life insurance, 208, 209, 210
    guaranteed renewable, 208
termination, 6, 7, 8, 9
termite certificate, 139, 140, 144, 152

third-party awards, 216, 217
title company, 126, 135
title insurance, 139, 147, 152
total disability, 220
traditional indemnity insurance, 169
transfer costs, 140, 142
TransUnion, LLC, 31

U

U.S.News and World Report, 183
umbrella insurance, 163, 167
unemployment insurance, 3, 15, 19
uninsured motorists coverage, 115, 117

V

vacation. *See annual leave*

W

waiver of premium provision, 220, 225
walk-through, 153
warranties, 231–237
    checklist for, 238, 239, 240
well yield test, 139, 140, 144, 145
whole life insurance, 208-211
wills, 48, 49
wire order, 43
withdrawal, 43
withholding, 55, 56
work description, 4
work environment, 15, 23
workers' compensation insurance, 3, 15, 19

About the Author

James M. Kramon, Esq., a graduate of George Washington and Harvard Law Schools, served as a federal prosecutor for four years and then opened his own law firm in Baltimore, Maryland. Over the past thirty years, his clients have included paupers and billionaires, mom-and-pop businesses and international corporations, and everything in between. Mr. Kramon has represented hospitals, construction companies, manufacturers of goods, providers of services, insurance companies, financial institutions, real estate developers, and government agencies.

Mr. Kramon has held various positions in bar associations and public-service organizations, and has taught courses at several law schools. In his over fifty articles and two previous books, Mr. Kramon has discussed a wide variety of legal and social issues. Mr. Kramon's work has been the subject of numerous television and radio broadcasts and it has been reviewed in major newspapers such as the Washington Post. Mr. Kramon has been listed in Who's Who in American Law and The Best Lawyers in America.

Further information concerning him may be found at:
www.kramonandgraham.com.